Item
not a
in wr
barco
at yo
Rene
Fines
Dam

KU-572-155

❤

Hi Lover

Published by Prion Books Ltd
an imprint of the Carlton Publishing Group
20 Mortimer Street
London W1T 3JW

Compilation copyright © 2005 Des MacHale
Design copyright © 2018 Carlton Publishing Group

All rights reserved. This book is sold subject to the
condition that it may not be reproduced, stored in a
retrieval system, or transmitted in any form or by any
means, electronic, mechanical, photocopying, recording
or otherwise, without the Publisher's prior consent.

ISBN 978-1-91161-001-4

A catalogue record of this book is available from the British
Library

Typeset by E-Type, Liverpool
Printed in the UK by CPI Group (UK) Ltd, Croydon, CR0 4Y

The material in this book was previously published as *Lovers' Wit*

Hi Lover

Des MacHale

PRION

Leabharlanna Poibli Chathair Baile Átha Cliath

Dublin City Public Libraries

Hi Lover

Sex, relationships, marriages and affairs have driven even the most level-headed individuals to sudden emotive outbursts of flushed-face anger, childlike excitement or hand-wringing despair.

In calmer moments, these matters of the heart can prompt amusing or cynical witticisms, or bemused, almost philosophical, mutterings about the absurdity of it all.

This book is a wonderful collection of quotations from the great lovers, the loved, the lost and the lecherous. With classic one-liners from a rich variety of humorists, writers, actors, politicians and musicians, ranging from Woody Allen to Anton Chekhov, Napoleon Bonaparte to Roy Brown, Denis Leary to Kathy Lette, and Rita Rudner to Mae West, this hilarious collection proves that when it comes to love, everybody has something to say…

Des MacHale is an Associate Professor at University College, Cork in Ireland and the author of forty humour books. He has been collecting witty remarks for thirty years and the established and long-running *Wit* series is a monument to his devotion – and great sense of humour.

The modern gentleman sees nothing fundamentally wrong with sex; it's good exercise and can round off an excellent day's shooting.

Tim Brooke-Taylor

The main trouble with women is that they will just not put the seat back up again.

Martin Clunes

Boyfriends need to understand that if women are worshipped, the world will be a better place.

Nicole Kidman

If an unmarried woman loses her equilibrium, she should try to fall on a millionaire.

W.C. Fields

My wife said: 'I want an explanation and I want the truth'. I said: 'Make up your mind'.

Henny Youngman

I like men – as a concept.

Jo Brand

My wife and I always hold hands. If I let go, she shops.

Rodney Dangerfield

Only the fear of my wife keeps me from a nervous breakdown.

George Bernard Shaw

If you find yourself unwilling to accept me, will you please pass this letter on to your sister Caroline.

Ralph Lovelace

The first time I had sex it lasted thirty seconds and boy was I embarrassed. I'm over it now though, I'm a lot quicker.

Duncan Norvelle

I hated my marriage, but I always had a great place to park.

Gerald Nachman

Earl Wilson asked me if I had ever been mistaken

for a man on the telephone. I replied 'No, darling, have you?'

Tallulah Bankhead

I'm not prudish but my mother told me never to enter a man's room in months with an 'R' in them.

Irene Dunne

She's really got it! I don't know exactly what it is, but if we could bottle it, we'd make a fortune.

Bob Hope

He has a heart of gold – only harder.

Dorothy Parker

Sex isn't necessary. You won't die without it, but you can die having it.

W. C. Fields

I change girlfriends every seven years, a habit I picked up from broken mirrors.

W. C. Fields

After a while marriage is a sibling relationship marked by occasional, rather regrettable episodes of incest.

Martin Amis

I prefer older men to younger men. Older men
can't run away so fast.

Jo Brand

I admit the most recent fight with my wife was my
fault. She said: 'What's on the TV?' and I said: 'Dust'.

Roy Brown

Feminism was established to allow unattractive
women easier access to the mainstream.

Rush Limbaugh

My husband said he needed more space, so I locked
him outside.

Roseanne Barr

No matter how many times I marry, I'll never
understand women.

Tony Randall

There's not much difference between kidnapping
and marrying. You get snatched from your parents
– but in marriage, nobody offers a reward.

Harry Davenport

Whenever I see a pretty girl I think to myself: 'Oh to be eighty again'.

George Burns

All men are animals but some make better pets than others.

Rita Rudner

I've been married to my wife for twenty years. The Black Death plague lasted only three years.

Roy Brown

No normal man ever fell in love after thirty when the kidneys begin to disintegrate.

H.L. Mencken

I concentrate on men and what horrible bastards they are. I don't suppose I'll ever run out of material.

Jo Brand

I worked in strip joints – but I never got my clothes off. People kept screaming: 'Don't do it, don't do it!'

Whoopi Goldberg

Will you take this woman to be your awful wedded wife?

Dylan Thomas

I'm still friends with all my ex's, apart from my husbands.

Cher

Come in girls and leave all hope behind.

Groucho Marx

If she was not a woman of the night then she was at very least a woman of the early morning.

Des MacHale

I am not a Don Juan. I am a very faithful man – I am faithful to my wife and I am faithful to my mistress.

Barbet Schroeder

Every two or three years I knock off for a while. That way I'm always the new girl in the whorehouse.

Robert Mitchum

Sarah Ferguson met Prince Andrew on the polo fields. But then, doesn't everybody?

Susan Barrantes

Being good in bed means I'm propped up with pillows and Mom brings me soup.

Brooke Shields

The husbands of very beautiful women belong to the criminal classes.

Oscar Wilde

The trouble with photographing beautiful women is that you never get into the dark room until after they've gone.

Yousuf Karsh

When the blind lead the blind, they both fall into matrimony.

George Farquhar

Gay marriage will never work. It's difficult enough when you have even one man in a marriage.

Graham Norton

He said it was artificial respiration, but now I find that I am to have his child.

Anthony Burgess

Sara could commit adultery at one end and weep for her sins at the other, and enjoy both operations at once.

Joyce Cary

Sex without love is an empty experience, but as empty experiences go, it's a pretty good empty experience.

Woody Allen

All this fuss about sleeping together. For physical pleasure I'd sooner go to my dentist any day.

Evelyn Waugh

It's so long since I've had sex I've forgotten who ties up whom.

Joan Rivers

The world is full of people who are ready to think the worst when they see a man sneaking out of the wrong bedroom in the middle of the night.

Will Cuppy

The majority of husbands remind me of an orangutang trying to play the violin.

Honoré de Balzac

It is well to write love letters. There are certain things it is not easy to ask your mistress for face to face – like money for instance.

Henri de Regnier

In the circles in which I move, sleeping with a woman does not constitute an introduction.

Virginia McLeod

I thought men like that shot themselves.

King George V

The quickest way to a man's heart is through his chest.

Roseanne Barr

If it wasn't for pickpockets and frisking at airports I wouldn't have any sex life at all.

Rodney Dangerfield

A lady is a woman who never shows her underwear unintentionally.

Lillian Day

I'm such a good lover because I practise a lot on my own.

Woody Allen

A eunuch is a man who has had his works cut out for him.

Robert Byrne

His designs were strictly honourable; that is to rob a lady of her fortune by way of marriage.

Henry Fielding

Sex between a man and a woman can be wonderful – provided you get between the right man and the right woman.

Woody Allen

What a blonde – she was enough to make a bishop kick a hole in a stained glass window.

Raymond Chandler

I blame my mother for my poor sex life. All she told me was: 'the man goes on top and the woman underneath'. For three years my husband and I slept in bunk beds.

Joan Rivers

The Love Bird is one hundred per cent faithful to his mate – as long as they are locked together in the same cage.

Will Cuppy

There is nothing in the world like the devotion of a married woman. It's a thing no married man knows anything about.

Oscar Wilde

I'd marry again if I found a man who had fifteen million dollars, would sign over half of it to me before the marriage, and guarantee he'd be dead within a year.

Bette Davis

Women are like elephants – everyone likes to look at them but no one likes to have to keep one.

W. C. Fields

My best birth control now is to leave the lights on.

Joan Rivers

Happiness is watching TV at your girlfriend's house during a power failure.

Bob Hope

Oh Lord, give me chastity, but do not give it yet.

St. Augustine

She was so ugly she could make a mule back away from an oat bin.

Will Rogers

Divorce is the sacrament of adultery.

Jean Guichard

What would men be without women? Scarce, sir, mighty scarce.

Mark Twain

Niagara Falls is the bride's second great disappointment.

Oscar Wilde

My love life is terrible. The last time I was inside a woman was when I visited the Statue of Liberty.

Woody Allen

How I wish that Adam had died with all his ribs in his body.

Dion Boucicault

I was actually the first birth from an inflatable woman.

Tony de Meur

I would rather go to bed with Lillian Russell stark naked than with Ulysses S. Grant in full military regalia.

Mark Twain

I think people should be free to engage in any sexual practices they choose – they should draw the line at goats though.

Elton John

A woman's mind is cleaner than a man's – that's because she changes it more often.

Oliver Herford

A man ought not to marry without having studied anatomy, and dissected at least one woman.

Honoré de Balzac

A man who marries his mistress creates a vacancy in the position.

James Goldsmith

Sex is an act which on sober reflection one recalls with repugnance and in a more elevated mood even with disgust.

Arthur Schopenhauer

The trees along the banks of the Royal Canal are more sinned against than sinning.

Patrick Kavanagh

My wife is the sort of woman who gives necrophilia a bad name.

Patrick Murray

It is bad manners to begin courting a widow before she gets home from the funeral.

Seumas MacManus

Drying a widow's tears is one of the most dangerous occupations known to man.

Dorothy Dix

Boy was my wife romantic! When I first met her she used to go round with a mattress strapped to her back.

Roy Brown

Marriage is like putting your hand into a bag of snakes in the hope of pulling out an eel.

Leonardo da Vinci

Sexual intercourse is a grossly overrated pastime; the position is undignified, the pleasure momentary, and the consequences utterly damnable.

Lord Chesterfield

Every woman is entitled to a middle husband she can forget.

Adela Rogers St. John

I had bad luck with both my wives. The first one left me and the second one didn't.

Patrick Murray

I go from stool to stool in singles bars hoping to get lucky, but there's never any gum under any of them.

Emo Philips

Men and women, women and men. It will never work.

Erica Jong

When a man steals your wife, there is no better revenge than to let him keep her.

Sacha Guitry

So little time, so many beautiful women to make love to.

Arturo Toscanini

I am the only man in the world with a marriage licence made out 'to whom it may concern'.

Mickey Rooney

Women's intuition is the result of millions of years of not thinking.

Rupert Hughes

My wife and I pondered for a while whether to take a vacation or get a divorce. We decided that a

trip to Bermuda is over in two weeks, but a divorce is something you always have.

Woody Allen

Splendid couple – slept with both of them.

Maurice Bowra

Men are superior to women. For one thing, men can urinate from a speeding car.

Will Durst

I'm dating a woman now who, evidently, is unaware of the fact.

Gary Shandling

She was stark naked except for a PVC raincoat, dress, net stockings, undergarments, shoes, rain hat, and gloves.

Keith Waterhouse

What is wrong with a little incest? It's both handy and cheap.

James Agate

I'm a wonderful housekeeper. Every time I get a divorce, I keep the house.

Zsa Zsa Gabor

She had once heard a semi-drunken peer say on TV that marriage without infidelity was like a salad without dressing.

Keith Waterhouse

Love is temporary insanity curable by marriage.

Ambrose Bierce

Love is the delusion that one woman differs from another.

H. L. Mencken

Bisexuality doubles your chances of a date on a Saturday night.

Woody Allen

Never make a task of pleasure, as the man said when he dug his wife's grave only three feet deep.

Seumas MacManus

It doesn't matter what you do in the bedroom as long as you don't do it in the streets and frighten the horses.

Mrs Patrick Campbell

She dresses to the left.

Patrick Murray

Love is the answer – but while you're waiting for the answer, sex raises some pretty good questions.

Woody Allen

My boyfriend and I broke up. He wanted to get married and I didn't want him to.

Rita Rudner

Ten men waiting for me at the door? Send one of them home, I'm tired.

Mae West

My wife is a sex object – every time I ask for sex, she objects.

Les Dawson

When a woman behaves like a man, why doesn't she behave like a nice man?

Edith Evans

A successful man is one who makes more money than his wife can spend. A successful woman is one who can find such a man.

Lana Turner

The people I'm furious with are the women's liberationists. They keep getting up on soapboxes and proclaiming women are brighter than men. That's true, but it should be kept quiet or it ruins the whole racket.

Anita Loos

There are only about twenty murders a year in London and not all are serious – some are just husbands killing their wives.

G.H. Hatherill

Sending your girl's love letters to your rival after he has married her is one form of revenge.

Ambrose Bierce

I sold the memoirs of my sex life to a publisher – they are going to make a board game out of it.

Woody Allen

He kissed me as though he was trying to clear the drains.

Alida Baxter

My wife Mary and I have been married for forty-seven years and not once have we had an argument

serious enough to consider divorce; murder, yes, but divorce, never.

Jack Benny

Some women's idea of being faithful is not having more than one man in bed at the same time.

Frederic Raphael

The main difference between men and women is that men are lunatics and women are idiots.

Rebecca West

Basically my wife was immature. I'd be at home in my bath and she'd come in and sink my boats.

Woody Allen

I've been married six months. She looks like a million dollars, but she only knows a hundred and twenty words and she's only got two ideas in her head. The other one is hats.

Eric Linklater

Love is just a dirty trick played on us to achieve the continuation of the species.

Somerset Maugham

A terrible thing happened to me last night again – nothing.

Phyllis Diller

I married beneath me. All women do.

Nancy Astor

I chased a woman for almost two years only to discover her tastes were exactly like mine – we were both crazy about girls.

Groucho Marx

Here's to woman! Would that we could fall into her arms without falling into her hands.

Ambrose Bierce

She said he proposed something on their wedding night that even her own brother wouldn't have suggested.

James Thurber

I like George and Harriet Grote. I like him; he's so ladylike. And I like her; she's such a perfect gentleman.

Sydney Smith

The chain of wedlock is so heavy that it takes two to carry it, sometimes three.

Alexandre Dumas

The ideal marriage consists of a deaf husband and a blind wife.

Padraig Colum

Every man should have the opportunity of sleeping with Elizabeth Taylor – and at the rate she's going, every man will.

Nicky Hilton

A nymphomaniac is a woman as obsessed with sex as the average man.

Mignon McLaughlin

My wife is as cold as the hairs on a polar bear's bum.

Les Dawson

It was so cold I almost got married.

Shelley Winters

We had gay burglars the other night. They broke in and rearranged the furniture.

Robin Williams

Despite my thirty years of research into the feminine soul, I have not yet been able to answer the great question that has never been answered: 'What does a woman want?'

Sigmund Freud

It is impossible to obtain a conviction for sodomy from an English jury. Half of them don't believe that it can physically be done, and the other half are doing it.

Winston Churchill

Women should have labels on their foreheads saying 'Government Health Warning: women can seriously damage your brains, genitals, current account, confidence, razor blades, and good standing among your friends'.

Jeffrey Bernard

You can lead a horticulture but you can't make her think.

Dorothy Parker

Sex is just poor man's polo.

Clifford Odets

I don't see so much of Alfred any more since he got so interested in sex.

Mrs Alfred Kinsey

Marriage is a ghastly public confession of a strictly private intention.

Ian Hay

If a pretty back view won't let you catch it up, it has probably got a horrible face.

Sydney Tremayne

If there is reincarnation, I'd like to come back as Warren Beatty's fingertips.

Woody Allen

Mankind and woman unkind.

Dick Diabolus

Lady Capricorn, he understood, was still keeping open bed.

Aldous Huxley

You know, of course, that the Tasmanians, who never committed adultery, are now extinct.

Somerset Maugham

All this divorce – when I meet a man now the first thing I think about is: 'Is this the sort of man I want my children to spend their weekends with?'

Rita Rudner

There is one thing I would break up over, and that is if she caught me with another woman. I wouldn't stand for that.

Steve Martin

I kissed my first woman and smoked my first cigarette on the same day: I have never had time for tobacco since.

Arturo Toscanini

If God had intended us to be nudists we would have been born with no clothes on.

Leonard Lyons

Sex is the invention of a very clever venereal disease.

David Cronenberg

When a woman, in the company of two men, addresses herself almost exclusively to one, you may be sure that she is busy beneath the table pressing the foot of the other.

Gian-Carlo Menotti

I am always looking for meaningful one-night
stands.

Dudley Moore

I never understood what he saw in her until I saw
her eating corn on the cob at the Caprice.

Coral Browne

It is not good for man to be alone. But oh my God,
what a relief.

John Barrymore

There are a number of mechanical devices which
increase sexual arousal, particularly in women.
Chief among these is the Mercedes-Benz 380SL
convertible.

P. J. O'Rourke

I wrote out a little list of questions for Pierre to put
to the Pope about our marriage problems.

Margaret Trudeau

I'll come to your room at five o'clock. If I'm late,
start without me.

Tallulah Bankhead

I can't for the life of me understand why people keep insisting that marriage is doomed. All five of mine worked out.

Peter de Vries

A woman is only a woman, but a good cigar is a smoke.

Rudyard Kipling

A woman without a man is like a fish without a bicycle.

Gloria Steinem

The happiest time of anyone's life is just after the first divorce.

J. K. Galbraith

Adultery? Why fool about with hamburger when you can have steak at home?

Paul Newman

I'm at the stage of life when if a girl says 'no' to me I'm profoundly grateful to her.

Woody Allen

There is nothing wrong with making love with the light on. Just make sure the car door is closed.

George Burns

She broke up with me when she found out I was sleeping with her.

Brian McCormick

Burt Reynolds once asked me to go out with him. I was in his room at the time.

Phyllis Diller

Love is a matter of chemistry – sex is simply physics.

G.M. Mark

She smoked 120 gaspers per day, swore like a fisherman, drank like a fish, and was promiscuous with men, women and Etonians.

Quentin Crisp

If you are bored with your present enemies and want to make some new ones, tell two of your women friends that they look alike.

Mignon McLaughlin

I once read an advertisement in a woman's magazine that went something like this:

'Do you want him to remember you and think of you when you're not there? Always wear the same perfume when you go out with him. The sense of smell is one of the greatest memory prodders. He'll learn to associate that scent with you and think of you every time he smells it, even on someone else.'

My God, does the woman think I'm a Labrador retriever?

Gilbert Harding

I have been to a funeral. I cannot describe to you the howl which the widow set up at proper intervals.

Charles Lamb

By all means marry; if you get a good wife, you'll become happy; if you get a bad one, you'll become a philosopher.

Socrates

Even if man could understand women he still wouldn't believe it.

A. W. Brown

Women now have the right to plant rolled-up
dollar bills in the jockstraps of steroid-sodden male
strippers.

Howard Ogden

I have never married – I find that if I come to like a
young woman well enough to marry her, I also find
that I have come to like her far too well to wish to see
her tied to an irritable bad-tempered old boor for life.

Gilbert Harding

Sex is God's joke on human beings.

Bette Davis

Making love to Marilyn Monroe was like kissing
Hitler.

Tony Curtis

My ultimate fantasy is to entice a man to my
bedroom, put a gun to his head, and say 'make
babies or die'.

Ruby Wax

Condemned female murderers get sheaves of offers
of marriage.

George Bernard Shaw

My notion of a wife at forty is that a man should be able to change her, like a bank note, for two twenties.

Douglas Jerrold

Women are an alien race of pagans set down among us. Every seduction is a conversion.

John Updike

I have climbed the ladder of success, wrong by wrong.

Mae West

Basically I wanted a woman who was an economist in the kitchen and a whore in bed. I wound up with a woman who was a whore in the kitchen and an economist in bed.

Geoffrey Gorer

Men come of age at sixty, women at fifteen.

James Stephens

I've been in love with the same woman for forty years – if my wife ever finds out, she'll kill me.

Henny Youngman

My parents had only one argument in forty-five years. It lasted forty-three years.

Cathy Ladman

The most difficult year of marriage is the one you're in.

Franklin P. Jones

Doris Day is as wholesome as a bowl of cornflakes and at least as sexy.

Dwight MacDonald

I am a double bagger. Not only does my husband put a bag over my face when we are making love but he also puts a bag over his own head in case my bag should fall off and he should have to look at me.

Joan Rivers

The height of ingratitude is the failure of Reno to erect a monument to Henry the Eighth.

Gerald F. Lieberman

That woman speaks eighteen languages and she can't say 'No' in any of them.

Dorothy Parker

An Arab and his camel are inseparable. It has been said that an Arab would give up his wife rather than give up his camel. Personally I haven't got a camel, but I think it's a great idea.

Groucho Marx

No man living knows more about women than I do – and I know nothing.

Seymour Hicks

Mr Ball? How very singular.

Thomas Beecham

I feel like a million tonight – but one at a time.

Mae West

Her grief lasted longer than I have known any widow's – three days.

Joseph Addison

I was with this girl the other night and from the way she was responding to my skilful caresses, you would have sworn she was conscious from the top of her head to the tag on her toes.

Emo Philips

It has been discovered experimentally that you can draw laughter from an audience anywhere in the world, of any class or race, simply by walking on to a stage, and uttering the words 'I am a married man'.

Ted Kavanagh

Philosophy is to the real world as masturbation is to sex.

Karl Marx

Of course prostitutes have babies – where do you think traffic wardens come from?

Dave Dutton

I have everything I had twenty years ago – except that now it's all lower.

Gypsy Rose Lee

I found a long grey hair on Kevin's jacket last night. If it's another woman's I'll kill him. If it's mine I'll kill myself.

Neil Simon

The reproduction of mankind is a great marvel and mystery. Had God consulted me in the matter, I should have advised Him to continue the generation of the species by fashioning them of clay.

Martin Luther

I'm not really a homosexual – I just help them out when they're busy.

Frank Carson

Girls are always running through my mind. They don't dare walk.

Andy Gibb

It was a man's world – then Eve arrived.

Richard Armour

Her eyes were bright brown – like a couple of cockroaches desperately swimming in two saucers of boiled rhubarb.

Gerald Kersh

I know a lot of people didn't expect our relationship to last – but we've just celebrated our two months anniversary.

Britt Eckland

My wife and I had words – but I never got to use mine.

Fibber McGee

She was a really bad-looking girl. Facially, she resembled Louis Armstrong's voice.

Woody Allen

If you want to know how old a woman is, ask her sister-in-law.

Edgar W. Howe

Sex at the age of eighty-four is a wonderful experience – especially the one in winter.

Milton Berle

A man is only as old as the women he feels.

Groucho Marx

Where would man be today if it weren't for women? In the Garden of Eden eating watermelon and taking it easy.

C. Kennedy

It's too bad that in most marriage ceremonies they don't use the word 'obey' any more. It used to lend a little humour to the occasion.

Lloyd Cory

Marry her! Impossible! You mean a part of her; he could not marry her all himself. There is enough of her to furnish wives for a whole parish. You might people a colony with her; or give an assembly with her; or perhaps take your morning's walk round her, always provided there were frequent resting-places, and you were in rude health.

Sydney Smith

Women have a much better time than men in this world. There are far more things forbidden to them.

Oscar Wilde

Recently, I've ventured into the mammal family – so that's good for my sex life.

Emo Philips

I wouldn't trust my husband with a young woman for five minutes, and he's been dead for twenty-five years.

Kathleen Behan

People in a temper often say a lot of silly things that they really mean.

Penelope Gilliat

I shrug my shoulders in despair at women who moan at the lack of opportunities and then take two weeks off as a result of falling out with their boyfriends.

Sophie Mirman

It should be a very happy marriage – they are both so in love with him.

Irene Thomas

The nearest I've been to a sexual experience lately is finding lipstick on a cafe cup.

Guy Bellamy

I have so little sex appeal my gynaecologist calls me 'sir'.

Joan Rivers

It had always seemed to Louis that a fundamental desire to take postal courses was being sublimated by other people into sexual activity.

Malcolm Bradbury

If I had been a woman I would be constantly pregnant because I simply cannot say no.

Robert Maxwell

My classmates would copulate with anything that moved, but I never saw any reason to limit myself.

Emo Philips

I do not believe in using women in combat, because females are too fierce.

Margaret Mead

Marriage is a great institution, but I'm not ready for an institution yet.

Mae West

If feminists were really serious about the movement, they would do something about their poor sisters who are forced to live on large alimony handouts from men they simply can't stand.

Lloyd Cory

When I have one foot in the grave, I will tell the whole truth about women. I shall tell it, jump into my coffin, pull the lid over me, and say 'Do what you like now.'

Leo Tolstoy

My love life is so bad I'm taking part in the world celibacy championships. I meet the Pope in the semi-finals.

Guy Bellamy

I once had a large gay following, but I ducked into an alleyway and lost him.

Emo Philips

The only time my wife and I had a simultaneous orgasm was when the judge signed the divorce papers.

Woody Allen

It was a mixed marriage. I'm human, he was a Klingon.

Carol Leifer

I've married a few people I shouldn't have, but haven't we all?

Mamie Van Doren

I'm busier than a whore working two beds.

Edgar W. Howe

If he ever makes love to me and I get to hear about it, his life won't be worth living.

Mae West

The only place men want depth in a woman is in her décolletage.

Zsa Zsa Gabor

Brains are never a handicap to a girl if she hides them under a see-through blouse.

Bobby Vinton

I have slept only with men I've been married to. How many women can make that claim?

Elizabeth Taylor

Some of the happiest marriages are when homosexuals marry upper-class ladies. The sex works, because the upper-class woman doesn't expect much, and the man just shuts his eyes and thinks of Benjamin Britten.

Jilly Cooper

Love is ideal. Marriage is real. The confusion of the two shall never go unpunished.

J. W. von Goethe

The poor wish to be rich, the rich wish to be happy, the single wish to be married, and the married wish to be dead.

Ann Landers

Of those that were born as men, all that were cowardly and spent their life in wrongdoing were transformed at the second birth into women. Such is the origin of women and of all that is female.

Plato

Every man is thoroughly happy twice in his life: just after he has met his first love, and just after he has left his last one.

H.L. Mencken

If you are married, it takes just one to make a quarrel.

Ogden Nash

I wanted to be a sex maniac but I failed the practical.

Robert Mitchum

As a young man I used to have four supple members and one stiff one. Now I have four stiff and one supple.

Henri Duc d'Aumale

A woman gives a man just two happy days: the day he marries her, and the day he buries her.

Hipponax

As a child of eight, Mr Trout had once kissed a girl of six under the mistletoe at a Christmas party, but there his sex life had come to an abrupt halt.

P. G. Wodehouse

The difference between divorce and legal separation is that a legal separation gives a husband time to hide his money.

Johnny Carson

I was at a gay nineties party the other night. All the men were gay and all the women were ninety.

Eric Morecambe

We sleep in separate rooms, we have dinner apart, we take separate vacations. We're doing everything we can to keep our marriage together.

Rodney Dangerfield

Women love men for their defects; if men have enough of them women will forgive them everything, even their gigantic intellects.

Oscar Wilde

When a couple decide to divorce, they should inform both sets of parents before having a party and telling all their friends. This is not only courteous but practical. Parents may be very willing to pitch in with comments, criticism and malicious gossip of their own to help the divorce along.

P. J. O'Rourke

I wasn't kissing your daughter, sir – I was just whispering in her mouth.

Chico Marx

Why does a woman work for ten years to change a man's habits and then complain that he's not the man she married?

Barbra Streisand

I like only two kinds of men – domestic and foreign.

Mae West

After we made love he took a piece of chalk and made an outline of my body.

Joan Rivers

One of my friends who is happily married has a husband so ugly she met him when a friend sent him over to her house to cure her hiccoughs.

Phyllis Diller

After my wife died, I put my mistress into cold storage for a bit.

H. G. Wells

When a man is a bit of a woman, one does like that bit to be a lady.

G. M. Young

We've just marked our tenth wedding anniversary on the calendar and threw darts at it.

Phyllis Diller

A husband should not insult his wife in public. He should insult her in the privacy of the home.

James Thurber

It takes a lot of experience for a girl to kiss like a beginner.

Joan Rivers

An open marriage is Nature's way of telling you that you need a divorce.

Ann Landers

What do I think of Volkswagens? I've been in bigger women.

Harry Kurnitz

There is no bigger fan of the opposite sex than me, and I have the bills to prove it.

Alan J. Lerner

Dammit, sir, it is your duty to get married. You can't be always living for pleasure.

Oscar Wilde

Women who can, do. Those who can't become feminists.

Bobby Riggs

There is just one remark to which there is no answer: 'what are you doing with my wife?'

Miguel de Cervantes

What part of 'no' don't you understand?

Rita Rudner

Not a soul dropped in to see me in my little cubicle in the office for days on end. I finally solved the problem by scratching my name off the door and replacing it with the legend Gents Room.

Dorothy Parker

To be able to turn a man out into the garden and tell him to stay there until the next meal, is every woman's dream.

Virginia Graham

When we got married my wife didn't have a rag on her back – but she's got plenty of them now.

Peter Eldin

Running after women never hurt anybody – it's catching them that does the damage.

Jack Davies

The great trick with a woman is to get rid of her while she thinks she's getting rid of you.

Søren Kierkegaard

All my wife has ever taken from the Mediterranean – from that whole vast intuitive culture – are four bottles of Chianti to make into lamps, and two china condiment donkeys named Sally and Peppy.

Peter Shaffer

Now that women are jockeys, baseball umpires, atomic scientists, and business executives, maybe someday they can master parallel parking.

Bill Vaughan

My wife's idea of double parking is to park her car on top of another car.

Shelley Berman

The longest sentence you can form with two words is 'I do'.

H.L. Mencken

She did have an illegitimate baby once but it was only a little one.

Frederick Marryat

Alas, she married another. They frequently do.
I hope she is happy, because I am.

Artemus Ward

Be wary, how you marry one that hath cast her
rider, I mean a widow.

James Howell

Almost any man can support the girl he marries, but
the problem is – what's he going to live on?

Joseph Salak

When we want to read the deeds that are done for
love, whither do we turn? To the murder columns.

George Bernard Shaw

Women are to be excluded from the eleventh
annual conker championships at Oundle. Our event
would be ridiculed if women competed.

Frank Elson

She could very well pass for forty-three, in the dusk
with a light behind her.

W. S. Gilbert

Annette had never been in love, although she was not without experience. She had been deflowered at seventeen by a friend of her brother on the suggestion of the latter. Nicholas would have arranged it when she was sixteen, only he needed her just then for a black mass.

Iris Murdoch

I have no time for sex. It gets in the way of the action.

Alistair MacLean

Never trust a husband too far, nor a bachelor too near.

Helen Rowland

I've never yet turned over a fig leaf that didn't have a price tag on the other side.

Saul Bellow

If you never want to see a man again say: 'I love you, I want to marry you, I want to have children'. They leave skid marks.

Rita Rudner

Every good painter who aspires to the creation of genuine masterpieces should first of all marry my wife.

Salvador Dali

A woman waits motionless until she is wooed. That is how the spider waits for the fly.

George Bernard Sha

Love is the delightful interval between meeting a girl and discovering she looks like a haddock.

John Barrymore

I never knew what real happiness was until I got married. And by then it was too late.

Max Kaufmann

Wives are people who think it's against the law not to answer the phone when it rings.

Ring Lardner

My fiancé and I are having a little disagreement. What I want is a big church wedding with bridesmaids and flowers and a no-expense-spared reception; and what he wants is to break off our engagement.

Sally Poplin

'Tis better to have loved and lost.

Alfred Tennyson

The biggest myth is that as you grow older, you gradually lose your interest in sex. This myth probably got started because younger people seem to want to have sex with each other at every available opportunity including traffic lights, whereas older people are more likely to reserve their sexual activities for special occasions such as the installation of a new Pope.

Dave Barry

This is good news; of memory, hearing, all the faculties – the last to leave us is sexual desire and the ability to make love. That means that long after we're wearing bifocals or hearing aids, we'll be making love. But we won't know with whom or why.

Jack Paar

A promiscuous person is someone who is getting more sex than you are.

Victor Lownes

Men who don't understand women fall into two groups – bachelors and husbands.

Jacques Languirand

A Casanova provides a useful special service – the best women like Rolls Royces should be delivered to the customer fully run-in.

Jilly Cooper

My wife – God bless her – was in labour for thirty-two hours, and I was faithful to her the entire time.

Jonathan Katz

Divorce is painful. There's an easy way to save yourself a lot of trouble. Just find a woman you hate and buy her a house.

Pat Paulsen

Outside every thin woman is a fat man trying to get in.

Katharine Whitehorn

If it's wet dry it. If it's dry wet it. Congratulations, you are now a gynaecologist.

Patrick Murray

She wore a low but futile décolletage.

Dorothy Parker

Anybody who says he can see through women is missing a lot.

Groucho Marx

I'm an intensely shy and vulnerable woman. My husband Norm has never seen me naked. Nor has he ever expressed the least desire to do so.

Dame Edna Everage

A man with pierced ears is better prepared for marriage. He has experienced pain and bought jewellery.

Rita Rudner

Only a flaw of fate prevented Vita Sackville-West from being one of nature's gentlemen.

Edith Sitwell

Women are a problem, but they are the kind of problem I enjoy wrestling with.

Warren Beatty

It takes a real man to wear make-up.

Rikki Rocket

The useless piece of flesh at the end of a penis is called a man.

Jo Brand

A loving wife will do anything for her husband except to stop criticising and trying to improve him.

J. B. Priestley

Of course I believe in safe sex – I've got a handrail around the bed.

Ken Dodd

To win a woman in the first place you must please her, then undress her, and then somehow get her clothes back on her; finally, so that she will let you leave her, you've got to antagonise her.

Jean Giradoux

The major achievement of the women's movement in the 1970s was the Dutch treat.

Nora Ephron

It's so tiring making love to women, it takes forever. I'm too lazy to be a lesbian.

Camille Paglia

You don't know how difficult it has been, being a closet heterosexual.

David Bowie

Nothing is more distasteful to me than that entire complacency and satisfaction which beam in the countenances of a new married couple.

Charles Lamb

When people say 'You're breaking my heart', they do in fact mean that you're breaking their genitals.

Jeffrey Bernard

Every man I meet wants to protect me. I can't figure out what from.

Mae West

The fulminations of the missionaries about sex in Listowel will have as little effect as the droppings of an underweight blackbird on the water-level of the Grand Coulee Dam.

Eamon Keane

The mini-skirt enables young ladies to run faster and because of it, they may have to.

John V. Lindsay

Brigands demand your money or your life –
women require both.

Samuel Butler

I have half a mind to get married – and that's all I
need.

Bob Phillips

My wife met me at the door wearing a see-through
negligee. Unfortunately, she was just coming
home.

Rodney Dangerfield

Teenage boys, goaded by their hormones, run in
packs like the primal horde. They have only a brief
season of exhilarating liberty between control by
their mothers and control by their wives.

Camille Paglia

Women's liberation will not be achieved until a
woman can become paunchy and bald and still
think she's attractive to the opposite sex.

Earl Wilson

A man's womenfolk, whatever their outward show
of respect for his merit and authority, always regard

him secretly as an ass, and with something akin to pity.

H. L. Mencken

Every woman needs at least three men: one for sex, one for money and one for fun.

Bess Myerson

Suburban Chicago is virgin territory for whorehouses.

Al Capone

On quiet nights, when I am alone, I like to run our wedding video backwards, just to watch myself walk out of the church a free man.

George Coote

Men should think again about making widowhood women's only path to power.

Gloria Steinem

If you think women are the weaker sex, try pulling the blankets back to your side.

Stuart Turner

No woman has ever shot her husband while he was doing the dishes.

George Coote

Never feel remorse for what you have thought about your wife; she has thought much worse things about you.

Jean Rostand

Edward Kennedy has just gone on his honeymoon. Now he'll be able to do something he's never been able to do before – check into a hotel under his own name.

Jay Leno

A woman's place is in the wrong.

James Thurber

Instead of getting married again, I'm going to find a woman I don't like and give her a house.

Lewis Grizzard

All the unhappy marriages come from husbands having brains. What good are brains to a man? They only unsettle him.

P. G. Wodehouse

A homely face and no figure have aided many a woman heavenward.

Minna Antrim

All the world loves a lover – unless he's in a telephone booth.

Dave Tomick

Pandora and I are in love! It is official! She told Claire Neilson, who told Nigel, who told me.

Adrian Mole

There is little wife-swopping in suburbia. It is unnecessary, the females all being so similar.

Richard Gordon

Funny how a wife can spot a blonde hair at twenty yards, yet miss the garage doors.

Corey Ford

If a man stays away from his wife for seven years, the law presumes the separation to have killed him; yet according to our daily experience, it might well prolong his life.

Charles Darling

The best way to get a husband to do anything is to suggest that he is too old to do it.

Shirley Maclaine

I can always find plenty of women to sleep with me but the kind of woman that is really hard for me to find is a typist who can read my writing.

Thomas Wolfe

For certain people, after fifty, litigation takes the place of sex.

Gore Vidal

A woman is the second most important item in a bedroom.

Paul Hogan

This book is dedicated to my brilliant and beautiful wife without whom I would be nothing. She always comforts and consoles, never complains or interferes, asks nothing and endures all. She also writes my dedications.

Albert Malvino

My sex life is now reduced to fan letters from an elderly lesbian who wants to borrow $800.

Groucho Marx

Marry me Dorothy and you'll be farting through silk.

Robert Mitchum

I met the ornithology correspondent of the *Irish Times*, a very prim and proper lady, one cold winter's afternoon and I said to her: 'How's the blue tits today, missus?'

Brendan Behan

A bore is a man in love with another woman.

Mary Poole

A man will marry a woman because he needs a mother he can communicate with.

Martin Mull

She is in love with her own husband – monstrous, what a selfish woman.

Jennie Churchill

A husband should tell his wife everything that he is sure she will find out anyway and before anybody else does.

Thomas Dewar

I'm quite happy with my mistress. She goes to bed with others because she loves them, but for money – only with me.

Ferenc Molnar

Telling a teenager the facts of life is like giving a fish a bath.

Arnold Glasow

Never despise what it says in the women's magazines: it may not be subtle but neither are the men.

Zsa Zsa Gabor

At eighty-two, I feel like a twenty-year-old, but unfortunately, there's never one around.

Milton Berle

Never trust a man with testicles.

Jo Brand

A very little wit is valued in a woman, as we are pleased with a few words spoken plain by a parrot.

Jonathan Swift

Marriage is but for a little while. It is alimony that is forever.

Quentin Crisp

There are four sexes: men, women, clergymen and journalists.

Somerset Maugham

The only way to get rid of cockroaches is to tell them you want a long-term relationship.

Jasmine Birtles

Men don't know anything about pain; they have never experienced labour, cramps or a bikini wax.

Nan Tisdale

How do I feel about men? With my fingers.

Cher

I have frequently been faithful to my wife.

Gerald Kennedy

In our family, we don't divorce our men – we bury them.

Ruth Gordon

The trouble is you can't live with men, but then you can't chop them into little pieces and boil the flesh off their bones, because that would be cooking.

Jenny Eclair

She was a freelance castrator.

James Thurber

It's a funny thing that when a man hasn't got anything on earth to worry about he goes off and gets married.

Robert Frost

The best part of married life is the fights. The rest is so-so.

Thornton Wilder

Man is the second strangest sex in the world.

Philip Barry

I love being married. It's so great to find the one special person you want to annoy for the rest of your life.

Rita Rudner

My husband claims to be a great sexual athlete, just because he always comes first.

Ellie Lane

In a world without men, there would be no crime and a lot of fat happy women.

Nicole Hollander

Marriage is a sort of friendship recognised by the police.

Robert Louis Stevenson

Sex is essentially just a matter of good lighting.

Noël Coward

Teenagers are God's punishment for having sex.

Patrick Murray

From where she parked the car it was just a short walk to the footpath.

Woody Allen

The Miss World Contest has always had its fair share of knockers.

Julia Morley

The only difference about being married is that you don't have to get out of bed to fart.

Jimmy Goldsmith

One of the advantages of living alone is that you don't have to wake up in the arms of a loved one.

Marion Smith

If you want sex, have an affair. If you want a relationship, buy a dog.

Julie Burchill

Once women made it public that they could do things better than men, they were of course forced to do precisely that. So now they have to be elected to political office and get jobs as officers of major corporations and so on, instead of ruling the world by batting their eyelids the way they used to.

P. J. O'Rourke

Sex hasn't been the same since women started to enjoy it.

Lewis Grizzard

Think of me as a sex symbol for the man who doesn't give a damn.

Phyllis Diller

My mother said it was simple to keep a man. You must be a maid in the living room, a cook in the kitchen and a whore in the bedroom. I said I'd hire the first two and take care of the bedroom bit myself.

Jerry Hall

The difference between sex and death is with death you can get to do it alone and nobody's going to make fun of you.

Woody Allen

This book is dedicated to all those men who betrayed me at one time or another, in the hope that they will fall off their motorcycles and break their necks.

Diane Wakoski

The hardest task in a girl's life is to prove to a man that his intentions are serious.

Helen Rowland

Of course a platonic relationship is possible, but only between a husband and wife.

Irving Kristol

Mrs. Williams has never yet let her husband finish a sentence since his 'I will', at Trinity Church, Plymouth Dock in 1782.

Patrick O'Brian

There is one thing women can never take away from men. We die sooner.

P. J. O'Rourke

They caught the first female serial killer, but she didn't kill the men herself. She gained access to their apartments, hid their remote controls and they killed themselves.

Elayne Boosler

I was the first woman to burn my bra – it took the fire department four days to put it out.

Dolly Parton

There are three intolerable things in life – cold coffee, lukewarm champagne and overexcited women.

Orson Welles

Marriage always demands the greatest understanding of the art of insincerity possible between two human beings.

Vicki Baum

I've been married so long I'm on my third bottle of Tabasco sauce.

Susan Vass

The night of our honeymoon my husband took one look and said, 'Is that all for me?'.

Dolly Parton

Teenage girls can get pregnant merely by standing downwind of teenage boys.

Dave Barry

A broken heart is what makes life so wonderful five years later, when you see the guy in the elevator and he is fat and smoking a cigar and saying 'long-time-no-see'. If he had not broken your heart you could not have that glorious feeling of relief.

Phyllis Battelle

If you had suggested to primitive man that they should watch women having babies, they would have laughed and tortured you for three or four days.

Dave Barry

I was into animal husbandry – until they caught me at it.

Tom Lehrer

Women dress alike all over the world; they dress to be annoying to other women.

Elsa Schiaparelli

The roses and raptures of vice are damned uncomfortable as you will soon find out. You have to get into such ridiculous positions.

John Mortimer

Whatever happened to the kind of love leech that lived in his car and dropped by once a month to throw up and use you for your shower? Now all the pigs want is a commitment.

Judy Tenuta

Her face was her chaperone.

Rupert Hughes

Some people ask the secret of our long marriage. We take time to go to a restaurant two times a week. A little candlelight, dinner, music and dancing. She goes on Tuesdays. I go Fridays.

Henny Youngman

My wife and I tried to breakfast together but we had to stop or our marriage would have been wrecked.

Winston Churchill

I'm the intelligent, independent-type woman. In other words, a girl who can't get a man.

Shelley Winters

I took up a collection for a man in our office but I didn't get enough money to buy one.

Ruth Buzzi

Elizabeth Taylor married Larry Fortensky, a man younger than her first wedding dress.

A.A. Gill

Meet me in the bedroom in five minutes and bring a cattle prod.

Woody Allen

Married! I can see you now, in the kitchen, bending over a hot stove, but I can't see the stove.

Groucho Marx

All women are stimulated by the news that any wife has left her husband.

Anthony Powell

There is so little difference between husbands you might as well keep the first.

Adela Rogers St. John

In Hollywood the girl throwing the bouquet at a wedding is just as likely to be the next one to marry as the girl who catches it.

Geraldine Page

Have you heard about the woman who stabbed her husband thirty-seven times? I admire her restraint.

Roseanne Barr

More husbands would leave home if they knew how to pack their suitcases.

Leopold Fetchner

Vittorio Gassman used to grab me in his arms, hold me close and tell me how wonderful he was.

Shelley Winters

Don't imagine you can change a man unless he's in nappies.

Jasmine Birtles

Open marriage is nature's way of telling you that you need a divorce.

Marshall Brickman

Never sleep with a man who has named his willy.

Jasmine Birtles

I belong to Bridegrooms Anonymous. Whenever I feel like getting married they send over a lady in housecoat and hair curlers to burn my toast for me.

Dick Martin

The first part of our marriage was very happy. Then, on the way back from the ceremony…

Henny Youngman

People keep asking me if I'll marry again. It's as if after you've had one car crash you want another.

Stephanie Beecham

Never get into a narrow double bed with a wide single man.

Quentin Crisp

When a man makes a woman his wife it's the highest compliment he can pay her and it's usually the last.

Helen Rowland

The only time a woman has a true orgasm is when she is shopping.

Joan Rivers

Remember men, we're fighting for this woman's honour; which is probably more than she ever did.

Groucho Marx

Being a woman is of interest only to aspiring male transsexuals. To actual women, it is simply a good excuse not to play football.

Fran Lebowitz

A man is only as old as the women he feels.

Groucho Marx

When he's late for dinner, I know he's either having an affair or is lying dead in the street. I always hope it's the street.

Jessica Tandy

I'll believe it when girls of twenty with money marry paupers turned sixty.

Elbert Hubbard

It's a pity that Marie Stopes's mother had not thought of birth control.

Muriel Spark

Love. Everyone says that looks don't matter, age doesn't matter, money doesn't matter. But I never met a girl yet who has fallen in love with an old ugly man who's broke.

Rodney Dangerfield

I'd much rather be a woman than a man. Women can cry, they can wear cute clothes – and they're the first to be rescued off sinking ships.

Gilda Radner

I want a man who is kind and understanding. Is that too much to ask of a billionaire?

Zsa Zsa Gabor

Infatuation is when you think he's as sexy as Robert Redford, as smart as Henry Kissinger, as noble as Ralph Nader, as funny as Woody Allen and as athletic as Jimmy Connors. Love is when you realise he's as sexy as Woody Allen, as smart as Jimmy Connors, as funny as Ralph Nader, as athletic as Henry Kissinger and nothing like Robert Redford – but you'll take him anyway.

Judith Viorst

I am not bald – my head is just a solar panel for a sex machine.

Telly Savalas

If women dressed for men, the clothes stores wouldn't sell much – just an occasional sun visor.

Groucho Marx

Anyone who calls it sexual intercourse can't possibly be interested in doing it. You might as well announce you're ready for lunch by proclaiming, 'I'd like to do some masticating and enzyme secreting'.

Allan Sherman

Sex is a bad thing because it crumples the bedclothes.

Jacqueline Onassis

Leaving sex to the feminists is like letting your dog vacation at the taxidermists.

Camille Paglia

I always run into strong women who are looking for weak men to dominate them.

Andy Warhol

Sleeping with Aldous Huxley was like being crawled over by slugs.

Nancy Cunard

My girlfriend told me she was seeing another man. I told her to rub her eyes.

Emo Philips

You know what I did before I got married?
Anything I wanted to.

Henny Youngman

If God had meant them to be lifted and separated,
He would have put one on each shoulder.

Victoria Wood

From best-sellers to comic books, any child who
hasn't acquired an extensive sex education by the
age of twelve belongs in remedial reading.

Will Stanton

The avowed purpose of pornography is to excite
sexual desire which is unnecessary in the case of the
young, inconvenient in the case of the middle aged
and impossible in the case of the old.

Malcolm Muggeridge

If you love a man, set him free. If he comes back, it
means he's forgotten his sandwiches.

Jasmine Birtles

I haven't heard of many girls being attracted by
poor old men.

Sophia Loren

In high school I would have killed for reliable information on the uterus. But having discussed it at length and seen full colour diagrams, I must say it has lost much of its charm, although I still respect it a great deal as an organ.

Dave Barry

Do I lift weights? Sure. Every time I stand up.

Dolly Parton

Boy, am I exhausted. I went on a double date the other night and the other girl didn't turn up.

Mae West

Your spouse should be attractive enough to turn you on. Anything more is trouble.

Albert Brooks

My wife and I have a great relationship. I love sex and she'll do anything to get out of the kitchen.

Milton Berle

I wanted to marry her ever since I saw the moonlight shining on the barrel of her father's shotgun.

Eddie Albert

A man without a woman is like a moose without a hat rack.

Arthur Marshall

There are men I could spend eternity with – but not this life.

Kathleen Norris

I learned about sex from my mother. I asked her where babies came from and she thought I said rabies. She said from a dog bite and a week later a lady on our block gave birth to triplets. I thought she had been bitten by a Great Dane.

Woody Allen

When I got back from my third honeymoon, I just couldn't understand why my husband wanted to come into the house with me. I was just about to say, 'Thanks for a nice time'.

Shelley Winters

Women now expect men to watch them have babies. This is called natural childbirth.

Dave Barry

It is said of me that when I was young, I divided my time impartially among wine, women and song. I deny this categorically. Ninety per cent of my interests were women.

Arthur Rubenstein

Between them the two men had a sperm count s maller than Cheltenham Ladies' College.

A. A. Gill

I knew Elizabeth Taylor when she didn't know where her next husband was coming from.

Anne Baxter

I am ninety-five. I still chase girls but I can't remember why.

George Burns

From my experience of life I believe my personal motto should be 'Beware of men bearing flowers'.

Muriel Spark

My computer dating bureau came up with a perfect gentleman. Still, I've got another three goes.

Sally Poplin

Having a baby is one of the hardest and most strenuous things known to man.

Anna Raeburn

I was married by a judge. I should have asked for a jury.

George Burns

After lovemaking, do you (a) go to sleep? (b) light a cigarette? (c) return to the front of the bus?

Joan Rivers

My wife finds it difficult to envisage me as the end product of millions of years of evolution.

Bob Barnes

Divorce comes from the old Latin word *divorcerum* meaning 'having your genitals torn out through your wallet'. And the judge said, 'All the money and we'll shorten it to alimony'.

Robin Williams

There is sex, but it's not what you think. Marvellous for the first fortnight. Then every Wednesday, if there isn't a good late night concert on Radio Three.

Malcolm Bradbury

Woman is a primitive animal who micturates once a day, defecates once a week, menstruates once a month, parturates once a year and copulates whenever she has the opportunity.

Somerset Maugham

When a woman on my show told me she had eighteen children because she loved her husband so much, I told her I loved my cigar too, but I took it out of my mouth once in a while.

Groucho Marx

If he tells you he likes black underwear, stop washing his pants.

Jasmine Birtles

I wouldn't mind being the last man on earth – just to see if all those girls were telling the truth.

Ronnie Shakes

When I fell in love with my wife, I thought those eyes, those lips, those chins. We had to go down the aisle in single file.

Roy Brown

She was looser than an MFI wardrobe.

Roy Brown

The thing that takes up the least amount of time and causes the most trouble is sex.

John Barrymore

My wife screams when she is having sex – especially when I walk in on her.

Roy Brown

At whatever stage you apologise to your wife, the answer is always the same – 'It's too late now'.

Denys Parsons

Women: you can't live with them and you can't get them to dress up in a skimpy Nazi costume and beat you with a warm squash.

Emo Philips

I like my lovers to be female, human and alive, but in a pinch, I'll take any two out of three.

Emo Philips

Love is just a system for getting someone to call you darling after sex.

Julian Barnes

A lot of girls go out with me just to further their careers – damn anthropologists.

Emo Philips

None of us can boast much about the morality of our ancestors: the records do not show that Adam and Eve were married.

Edgar W. Howe

One of the most difficult things in this world is to convince a woman that even a bargain costs money.

Edgar W. Howe

If your husband has difficulty in getting to sleep, the words, 'We need to talk about our relationship' may help.

Rita Rudner

The worst aspect of marriage is that it makes a woman believe that other men are just as easy to fool.

H. L. Mencken

It isn't premarital sex if you have no intention of getting married.

Matt Barry

A man should marry only a very pretty woman in case he ever wants some other man to take her off his hands.

Sacha Guitry

Men have higher body temperatures than women. If your heating goes out in winter, I recommend sleeping next to a man. Men are basically portable heaters that snore.

Rita Rudner

I'm a great lover, I'll bet.

Emo Philips

I never met a woman that, if you got to know her, didn't want to squeeze your pimples.

David Arnason

Some women think bikinis are immodest, while others have beautiful figures.

Olin Miller

Women inspire men to great undertakings and then distract them from carrying them out.

Oscar Wilde

My dog was my only friend. I told my wife that every man needs at least two friends, so she bought me another dog.

Henny Youngman

After a man is married he has the legal right to deceive only one woman.

Edgar W. Howe

When my jokes are explained to her and she has the leisure to reflect on them, she laughs very heartily.

Sydney Smith

Changeable women are more endurable than monotonous ones; they are sometimes murdered but rarely deserted.

George Bernard Shaw

Few men know how to kiss well – fortunately, I've always had time to teach them.

Mae West

A widower enjoys a second wife as much as a widow enjoys her husband's life insurance.

Edgar W. Howe

I would like to announce that the notice I put in this newspaper last week was in error. I will be responsible for any debts incurred by my wife. And I will start paying them as soon as I get out of hospital.

Henny Youngman

The penalty for getting the woman is that you must keep her.

Lionel Strachey

Women have a hard enough time in this world – telling them the truth would be too cruel.

H. L. Mencken

When a man goes crazy, his wife is the first to know it and the last to admit it.

Edgar W. Howe

A man finds it awfully hard to lie to the woman he loves – the first time.

Helen Rowland

If I ever marry, it will be on a sudden impulse – as a man shoots himself.

H. L. Mencken

When you consider what a chance women have to poison their husbands, it's a wonder there isn't more of it done.

Kin Hubbard

In my day, hot pants were something we had, not wore.

Bette Davis

If you haven't seen your wife smile at a traffic cop, you haven't seen her smile her prettiest.

Kin Hubbard

A woman who takes her husband about with her everywhere is like a cat that goes on playing with a mouse long after she's killed it.

H. H. Munro

An elderly actress I once knew had a claim to fame. She had been seduced by a man with a wooden leg in the Garden of Gethsemane.

Steve Race

I was walking down Soho when a young lady asked if I would sleep with her for fifty pounds. Well, I wasn't tired, but I thought the money would come in handy.

Harry Scott

If you think you're in love just think of him sitting on the lavatory. If you still love him, marry him.

Jean Boht

In the Forties, to get a girl, you had to be a GI or a jock. In the Fifties, to get a girl, you had to be Jewish. In the Sixties, to get a girl, you had to be black. In the Seventies, to get a girl, you have to be a girl.

Mort Sahl

My girlfriend told me I was immature emotionally, sexually and intellectually. I said, 'Yes, but in what other ways?'

Woody Allen

I got married the second time in the same way that when a murder is committed, crackpots turn up at the police station to confess the crime.

Delmore Schwartz

A wedding is a funeral where you smell your own flowers.

Eddie Cantor

I went into a feminist bookstore the other day. I looked more female than anybody in there.

Clint Eastwood

If her dress had pockets my wife would look like a pool table.

Rodney Dangerfield

Lulubelle, it's you! I didn't recognise you standing up.

Groucho Marx

I must marry – if only to get to bed at a reasonable hour.

Benjamin Constant

Marriage is when a woman asks a man to remove his pyjamas because she wants to send them to the laundry.

Albert Finney

A woman told me she would fulfil my ultimate fantasy for £100. I asked her to paint my house.

Sean O'Bryan

Laugh and the world laughs with you. Snore and you sleep alone.

Anthony Burgess

When we were dating we spent most of our time talking about sex – why I couldn't do it, where we could do it, were her parents going to go out so we could do it. Now that we're married, we've got nothing to talk about.

Daniel Stern

My girlfriend has lovely coloured eye. I particularly like the blue one.

Harry Scott

I wish I had the experience that some woman had killed herself for love of me. The women who have admired me have all insisted on living on, long after I have ceased to care for them.

George Sanders

I've trusted men all my life and I've never been deceived yet – except by my husbands and they don't count.

Mary Boland

I knew I was in love. First of all, I was very nauseous.

Woody Allen

I was incredible in bed last night. I never once had to sit up and consult the manual.

Woody Allen

The charms of a passing woman are usually in direct proportion to the speed of her passing.

Marcel Proust

I've often been chased by women but never while I was awake.

Bob Hope

Women; can't live with them, can't bury them in the back yard without the neighbours seeing.

Sean Williamson

When authorities warn you of the dangers of sex,

there is an important lesson to be learned. Do not have sex with the authorities.

Matt Groening

Men should be like Kleenex – soft, strong and disposable.

Cher

The three words you don't want to hear, while making love are 'Honey I'm home'.

Ken Hammond

An eighty-year-old friend of mine has just returned from his honeymoon with his eighteen-year-old bride. He described it as like trying to force a marshmallow into a piggy bank.

Keith Waterhouse

Everyone should be married. A bachelor's life is no life for a single man.

Sam Goldwyn

The time you spend grieving over a man should never exceed the amount of time you actually spent with him.

Rita Rudner

Don't have sex man. It leads to kissing and pretty soon you've got to talk to them.

Steve Martin

Women complain about premenstrual syndrome, but I think of it as the only time of the month I can be myself.

Roseanne Barr

Like most men, I am consumed with desire whenever a lesbian gets within twenty feet.

Taki

She was so sweet that we just walked in the park and I was so touched by her that, after fifteen minutes, I wanted to marry her and, after half an hour, I completely gave up the idea of snatching her purse.

Woody Allen

If a woman insists on being called Ms, ask her if that stands for miserable.

Russell Bell

Give a man a free hand and he'll run it all over you.

Mae West

You should always be missing some buttons. It's part of your boyish bachelor charm. Many a woman has sat down on the living room couch to sew a button and has wound up doing something more interesting on another piece of furniture elsewhere in the room.

P. J. O'Rourke

Women asserted that they would not be dictated to but then went out and became stenographers.

G. K. Chesterton

I don't know the question, but sex is definitely the answer.

Woody Allen

They were not so much her private parts as her public parts.

Alan Bennett

Golf and sex are the only things you can enjoy without being any good at them.

Jimmy Demaret

There was not much wrong with Virginia Woolf except that she was a woman.

Germaine Greer

During my army medical, they asked me if I was homosexual. I said I wasn't but I was willing to learn.

Bill Murray

When I eventually met Mr Right, I had no idea his first name was 'Always'.

Rita Rudner

Under twenty-one women are protected by law; over sixty-five they're protected by nature; anything in-between is fair game.

Cary Grant

There is at least one fool in every married couple.

Henry Fielding

Women are nothing but machines for producing children.

Napoleon Bonaparte

Sex is one of the most wholesome, beautiful and natural things that money can buy.

Steve Martin

When thou goest to woman, take thy whip.

Friedrich Nietzsche

You have to go back to the Children's Crusade in AD 1212 to find as unfortunate and fatuous attempt at manipulated hysteria as the Women's Liberation Movement.

Helen Lawrenson

I was asked if I would support the '18' compromise in the coming debate on the age of homosexual consent in the House of Lords, but I must have been reading the bill upside down because I thought it said '81', which did seem most unfair.

William Temple

The others were only my wives. But you my dear, my fifth wife, will also be my widow.

Sacha Guitry

I had the upbringing a nun would envy. Until I was

fifteen I was more familiar with Africa than my own body.

Joe Orton

My wife's hands are so beautiful that I'm going to have a bust made of them.

Sam Goldwyn

Any married man should forget his mistakes – no use two people remembering the same thing.

Duane Dewel

A married couple are well suited when both partners usually feel the need for a quarrel at the same time.

Jean Rostand

A man should be taller, older, heavier, uglier and hoarser than his wife.

Edgar W. Howe

If you cannot have your dear husband for a comfort and a delight, for a crosspatch, for a sofa, chair or a hotwater bottle, one can use him as a 'Cross to be Borne'.

Stevie Smith

She is a peacock in everything but beauty.

Oscar Wilde

Another reason girls talk earlier than boys is breastfeeding. Boys would rather breastfeed than talk because they know they won't be getting that close again for another fifteen years.

Paul Seaburn

I wouldn't be caught dead marrying a woman old enough to be my wife.

Tony Curtis

You're getting old if you discuss the facts of life with your children and you get slapped by your wife when you attempt to try out some of the things they told you.

Russell Bell

Men have simple needs. They can survive the whole weekend with only three things: beer, boxer shorts, and batteries for the remote control.

Diana Jordan

When I was your age, I had been an inconsolable

widower for three months, and was already paying my addresses to your admirable mother.

Oscar Wilde

Ask a toad what is beauty? A female with two great round eyes coming out of her little head, a large flat mouth, a yellow belly and a brown back.

Voltaire

A woman voting for divorce is like a turkey voting for Christmas.

Alice Glynn

Before we make love, my husband takes a painkiller.

Joan Rivers

If you want a good sex life the answer is communication. If you're making love to your partner, tell her.

Ivor Dembina

I have no boobs whatsoever. On my wedding night my husband said, 'Let me help you with those buttons' and I told him, 'I'm completely naked'.

Joan Rivers

Hanging on to a bad relationship is like chewing gum after the flavour has gone.

Rita Rudner

I have never married because I cannot mate in captivity.

Gloria Steinem

Conventional intercourse is like squeezing jam into a doughnut.

Germaine Greer

Breathes there a man with hide so tough, who says two sexes aren't enough?

Sameul Hoffenstein

Men carry their brains lower than women do, so when they're scratching their crotches, they're not being gross – they're just thinking.

Diana Jordan

The best way to remember your wife's birthday is to forget it once.

Joseph Cossman

Even the most respectable woman has a complete set of clothes in her wardrobe ready for a possible abduction.

Sacha Guitry

I would rather see a woman die, any day, than see her happy with someone else.

Pablo Picasso

There comes a moment in the day, when you have written your pages in the morning, attended to your correspondence in the afternoon, and have nothing further to do. Then comes the hour when you are bored; that's the time for sex.

H.G.Wells

Nowadays I chase girls only if they're going downhill.

George Burns

I'm all for women's rights – and for their lefts too.

Groucho Marx

To please my wife, I decided to get in touch with my feminine side. Now I've got a yeast infection.

Bob Delaney

You can tell how long a couple has been married by whether they are on their first, second or third bottle of Tabasco sauce.

Bruce R. Bye

Men aren't attracted to me by my mind. They are attracted to me by what I don't mind.

Gypsy Rose Lee

A sexagenarian, at his age, I think that's disgusting.

Gracie Allen

I save a fortune on plastic surgery. I just always turn the lights out.

Phyllis Diller

The secret of a successful marriage is not to be at home too much.

Colin Chapman

We have a saying in Russia, 'Women are like buses'. That's it.

Yakov Smirnoff

My girlfriend said to me in bed the other night,

'You're a pervert'. I said to her: 'That's a big word for a girl of nine'.

Emo Philip

When I was told that by the year 2100 women would rule the world, I replied 'Still?'

Winston Churchill

In my house I'm the boss. My wife is just the decision maker.

Woody Allen

It was partially my fault that we got divorced. I tended to put my wife under a pedestal.

Woody Allen

Conrad Hilton gave me a very generous divorce settlement. I wound up with 5000 Gideon Bibles.

Zsa Zsa Gabor

The essential difference between men and women is that if you ask a woman how she feels, sooner or later you'll hear about every relationship she's ever been in. Ask a man what he feels and he'll tell you he feels like a pizza.

Diana Ford

Is sex dirty? Only if it's done right.

Woody Allen

Don't knock masturbation – it's sex with someone you love.

Woody Allen

Marrying for love is a very recent idea. In the old country, they didn't marry for love. A man married a woman because he needed an extra mule.

Woody Allen

The appropriate age for marriage is about eighteen for girls and thirty-seven for men.

Aristotle

A wise woman will always let her husband have her way.

Richard Brinsley Sheridan

I once read about a species of fish wherein the male is much smaller than the female, and when he mates with her, he becomes permanently stuck to her, and she sort of absorbs him until he is actually part of her body, just an appendage of the female, kind of

like whoever is currently married to Elizabeth
Taylor.

Dave Barry

I've finally figured out that being male is the same
thing more or less, as having a personality disorder.

Carol Shields

If thee marries for money, thee surely will earn it.

Ezra Bowen

Marriage is the most advanced form of warfare in
the modern world.

Malcolm Bradbury

I asked her if she was doing anything on Saturday
night and she told me she was committing suicide. So
I asked her if she was doing anything on Friday night.

Woody Allen

I had a love–hate relationship with one of my
husbands. He loved me, I hated him.

Zsa Zsa Gabor

Have I ever paid for sex? Only emotionally.

Lee Hurst

James Hunt used to write me love letters from all over the world. Well, not actually love letters. They were more like technical reports on his car.

Taormina Rich

Beware of the man who picks your dresses; he wants to wear them.

Erica Jong

A man and wife should never have it in their power to hang one another.

George Farquhar

I don't know if my first experience was heterosexual or homosexual because I was too polite to ask.

Gore Vidal

A lady, if surprised by melancholy, might go to bed with a chap, once; or a thousand times if consumed by passion. But twice my dear fellow, twice, a lady might think she'd been taken for a tart.

Tom Stoppard

My wife doesn't care what I do when I'm away as long as I don't have a good time.

Lee Trevino

Marriage is a matter of give and take. You better give it to her, or she'll take it anyway.

Joey Adams

My wife got the house, the car, the bank account, and if I marry again and have children, she gets them too.

Woody Allen

'Tis safest in matrimony to begin with a little aversion.

Richard Brinsley Sheridan

Have you ever started dating someone because you were too lazy to commit suicide?

Judy Tenuta

I gave my beauty and youth to men. I am going to give my wisdom and experience to animals.

Brigitte Bardot

Women run everything. The only thing I have decided in my house over the last twenty years is to recognise Angola as an independant state.

Brian Clough

I believe it is possible to obtain a divorce in the United States on the grounds of incompatibility. If that is true, I am surprised there are any marriages left in the United States.

G.K. Chesterton

Joan Collins unfortunately can't be with us tonight. She's busy attending the birth of her next husband.

John Parrott

Women are called the opposite sex because when you want to do anything they want to do the opposite.

Corey Ford

Anyone making love to Germaine Greer should have his guide dog confiscated and be awarded the Victoria Cross.

Bernard Manning

It is relaxing to go out with my ex-wife because she already knows I'm an idiot.

Warren Thomas

I told my wife the truth. I told her I was seeing a psychiatrist. Then she told me the truth – she was seeing a psychiatrist, two plumbers and a bartender.

Rodney Dangerfield

Never marry a man with a big head. Because you're going to give birth to that man's child and you want a baby with a narrow head.

Jilly Goolden

A 'Bay Area Bisexual' told me I didn't quite coincide with either of her desires.

Woody Allen

Whatever else can be said about sex, it cannot be called a dignified performance.

Helen Lawrenson

I was so flat I used to put 'x's' on my chest and write 'you are here'.

Joan Rivers

Zsa Zsa Gabor got married as a one-off and it was so successful she turned it into a series.

Bob Hope

My thirteenth wife cried and the judge wiped her tears with my chequebook.

Tommy Manville

I'm glad I'm not bisexual – I couldn't stand being rejected by men as well as women.

Bernard Manning

They kept mistresses of such dowdiness they might almost have been mistaken for wives.

Robertson Davies

'Tis better to have loved and lost than never to have lost at all.

Samuel Butler

There are three kinds of bachelors: the kind that must be driven into matrimony with a whip; the kind that must be coaxed with sugar; and the kind that must be blindfolded and backed into the shafts.

Helen Rowland

The only real argument for marriage is that it remains the best method for getting acquainted.

Heywood Brown

Alas! In choosing a husband, it seems that you've always got to decide between something tame and uninteresting, like a goldfish and something wild and fascinating like a mountain goat.

Helen Rowland

It is not true that I had nothing on. I had the radio on.

Marilyn Monroe

I feel cheated, never being able to know what it's like to get pregnant, carry a child and breastfeed.

Dustin Hoffman

My true friends have always given me that supreme proof of devotion; a spontaneous aversion for the man I loved.

Colette

When I'm good, I'm very very good, but when I'm bad, I'm better.

Mae West

I like to wake up feeling a new man.

Jean Harlow

The difference between a man and a woman I cannot conceive.

John Mahaffy

I was introduced to a beautiful young lady as a man in his nineties. Early nineties, I insisted.

George Burns

My girlfriend turns twenty-one next week. In honour of the event I'm going to stop bathing her in the sink.

Jerry Seinfeld

Women, you can't live with them and sheep can't cook.

Emo Philips

There's nothing like good food, good wine and a bad girl.

Robin Williams

I'm not a breast man. I'm a breast person.

John Wilson

I hate a woman who seems to be hermetically sealed in the lower regions.

H. Allen Smith

When a man makes a woman his wife, it's the highest compliment he can pay her, and it's usually the last.

Helen Rowland

I like younger women. Their stories are shorter.

Tom McGuane

The only thing my husband and I have in common is that we were married on the same day.

Phyllis Diller

I don't know what the Left is doing, said the Right Hand, but it looks fascinating.

James Broughton

I bequeath to my wife the sum of one shilling for a tram fare so she can go somewhere and drown herself.

Francis Lord

Where did I first kiss my present partner? On her insistence.

Daire O'Brien

I used to be Snow White, but I drifted.

Mae West

I haven't spoken to my wife for over a month. We haven't had a row – it's just that I'm afraid to interrupt her.

Les Dawson

I dislike the idea of wives about a house: they accumulate dust. Besides, so few of the really nice women in my set could afford to marry me.

H.H. Munro

One hard and fast rule of my sex life is only one willy in the bed at a time.

A.A. Gill

Most women are not so young as they are painted.

Max Beerbohm

All that this humourless document, the Kinsey
Report, proves is:

(a) that all men lie when they are asked about their
    adventures in amour, and

(b) that pedagogues are singly naive and credulous
    creatures.

H.L. Mencken

Every time Magda Goebbels saw Hitler, her ovaries
rattled.

Peter Watson

Never try to impress a woman: because if you do
she'll expect you to keep up the standard for the rest
of your life. And the pace, my friends, is devastating.

W.C. Fields

If a woman has had more than three husbands, she
poisons them; avoid her.

William Maguire

The only time a woman really succeeds in changing
a man is when he is a baby.

Natalie Wood

If a tree falls in the woods and there is nobody there

to hear it fall, does it still make a sound? And if a man speaks and there is no woman there to correct him, is he still wrong?

Camille Paglia

I'm too shy to express my sexual needs except over the phone to people I don't know.

Gary Shandling

Women should never wear anything that panics the cat.

P.J. O'Rourke

Lord Ormsby, 85, has just married Lady Astorite, 18. The groom's gift to the bride was an antique pendant.

Peter Shaw

Did I sleep with her? Not a wink, father, not a wink.

Brendan Behan

When men are angry and upset, they rebel by hurting others; when women are angry and upset, they rebel by hurting themselves: bulimia, anorexia,

self-mutilation, suicide and getting married to members of the Windsor family.

Julie Burchill

A bridegroom is a man who has spent a lot of money on a suit that no one notices.

Josh Billings

A girl should marry for love, and keep on marrying until she finds it.

Zsa Zsa Gabor

A man can sleep around, no questions asked, but if a woman makes nineteen or twenty mistakes, she's a tramp.

Joan Rivers

I couldn't tell if the streaker was a man or a woman because it was wearing no clothes.

Yogi Berra

I remember the first time I had sex – I still have the receipt.

Groucho Marx

The only females that pursue me are mosquitoes.

Emo Philips

The way to tell if a man is sexually excited is if he's breathing.

Jo Brand

Everybody considers her very beautiful, especially from the neck down.

Damon Runyon

Just two more laser treatments and the 'Rosanne' tattoo is gone from my chest.

Tom Arnold

The problem which confronts homosexuals is that they set out to win the love of a 'real' man. If they succeed, they fail. A man who goes with other men is not what they would call a real man.

Quentin Crisp

If love means never having to say you're sorry, then marriage means always having to say everything twice.

Estelle Getty

Before I met my husband, I'd never fallen in love.
I stepped in it a few times.

Rita Rudner

A man can have two, maybe three, love affairs while
he's married. But three is the absolute maximum.
After that you're cheating.

Yves Montand

A woman will sometimes forgive the man who tries
to seduce her, but never the man who misses the
opportunity when offered.

Charles de Talleyrand

I can provide temporary relief for nymphomaniacs.

Larry Lee

I am told he has fallen in love. Against whom?

Abed Adler

A wife lasts only for the length of the marriage, but
an exwife is there for the rest of your life.

Jim Samuels

I have difficulty in avoiding the persistent attentions of ladies of the street. It's a case of the tail dogging the wag.

S. J. Perelman

Have the florist send some roses to Mrs Upjohn and write, 'Emily, I love you', on the back of the bill.

Groucho Marx

When widows exclaim loudly against second marriages, I would always lay a wager, that the man, if not the wedding day is absolutely fixed upon.

Henry Fielding

I can honestly say that I always look on Pauline as one of the nicest girls I was ever engaged to.

P. G. Wodehouse

Only one man in a thousand is a leader of men – the other nine hundred and ninety-nine follow women.

Groucho Marx

The purpose of sexual intercourse is to get it over with as long as possible.

Steven Max Singer

I have a tremendous sex drive. My boyfriend lives forty miles away.

Phyllis Diller

It is only rarely that one can see in a little boy the promise of a man, but one can almost always see in a little girl the threat of a woman.

Alexandre Dumas

The proliferation of massage establishments in London in the last few years appears to indicate a dramatic increase in muscular disorders amongst the male population.

Evelyn Waugh

I have such poor vision I can date anybody.

Gary Shandling

I would go out with women my age, but there are no women my age.

George Burns

In biblical times, a man could have as many wives as he could afford. Just like today.

Abigail Van Buren

I don't know how much it costs to get married –
I'm still paying for it.

Les Dawson

God gave men a penis and a brain, but not enough
blood to use both at the same time.

Robin Williams

A married couple playing cards together is just a
fight that hasn't started yet.

George Burns

The fella that puts off marrying until he can support
a wife ain't much in love.

Kin Hubbard

Guns don't kill people; husbands that come home
early kill people.

Don Rose

I once placed an ad in the personal columns of
Private Eye saying that I wanted to meet a rich well-
insured widow with a view to murdering her. I got
forty-eight replies.

Spike Milligan

I am not against hasty marriages, where a mutual flame is fanned by an adequate income.

Wilkie Collins

They say that the daughter-in-law of the Spanish Ambassador is not ugly, and has as good a set of teeth as one can have, when one has but two and those black.

Horace Walpole

I bank at this women's bank. Everybody is in the red three or four days a month.

Judith Carter

I haven't had any open marriages, though quite a few have been ajar.

Zsa Zsa Gabor

The most romantic thing any woman ever said to me in bed was 'Are you sure you're not a cop?'

Larry Brown

As Major Denis Bloodnok exclaimed when told there were only two sexes: 'It's not enough, I say'.

Albert Hall

Fat generally tends to make a man a better husband. His wife is happy in the knowledge she is not married to a woman chaser. Few fat men chase girls, because they get winded so easily.

Hal Boyle

It wasn't exactly a divorce – I was traded.

Tim Conway

By love, of course, I refer to romantic love – the love between man and woman, rather than between mother and child, or a boy and his dog, or two head waiters.

Woody Allen

I have little experience of marriage, having been married only once.

Oscar Wilde

There is a way of transferring funds that is even faster than electronic banking. It's called marriage.

James McGavran

If you have to ask if somebody is male or female, don't.

Patrick Murray

Transsexuals always seem to feel that they have been Shirley Bassey trapped inside a man's body rather than an assistant from an Oxfam Shop trapped inside a man's body.

Paul Hoggart

I require only three things of a man. He must be handsome, ruthless and stupid.

Dorothy Parker

I told him that I would give him a call but what I really meant was that I would rather have my nipples torn off by wild dogs than see him again.

Rita Rudner

Men are people, just like women.

Fenella Fielding

What attracted me to Lytton in the first place was his knees.

Carrington Strachey

If a woman hasn't met the right man by the time she's twenty-four, she may be lucky.

Deborah Kerr

You remember your first mountain in much the same way as you remember having your first sexual experience, except that climbing doesn't make as much mess and you don't cry for a week if Ben Nevis forgets to phone the next morning.

Muriel Gray

A woman will lie about anything, just to stay in practice.

Phillip Marlowe

She was the finest woman that ever walked the streets.

Mae West

When women are depressed they either eat or go shopping. Men invade another country.

Elayne Boosler

Love is the one game that is never called off on account of darkness.

Tom Masson

It is better taste somehow that a man should be unfaithful to his wife away from home.

Barbara Pym

Advice to young men about to marry – don't.

Mister Punch

Bigamy is one way of avoiding the painful publicity of divorce and the expense of alimony.

Oliver Herford

Women – you can't live with them and you can't live with them.

Marsh Mellow

Amnesia is a condition that enables a woman who has gone through labour to have sex again.

Fran Lebowitz

You're so gorgeous, I bet even the bags under your eyes are made by Gucci.

Kenny Everett

My girlfriend tells me I'm a pearl – the result of constant irritation.

Jim Davis

Norman Mailer likes women so much he likes even Hillary Clinton.

Paul Johnson

No one will ever win the battle of the sexes; there's too much fraternising with the enemy.

Henry Kissinger

Dickie Mountbatten loved to look at the menu, but rarely ate the main course.

Douglas Fairbanks Jr.

Some people are just not cut out to be married – like men.

Jimmy Tarbuck

I saw this nature show on TV about how the male elk douses himself with urine to smell sweeter to the opposite sex. What a coincidence.

Jack Handey

O what a tangled web we weave when first we practise to conceive.

Don Herold

I don't think their marriage will last. When the groom said 'I do', the bride said 'Don't use that tone of voice with me'.

Gary Apple

She didn't mean to get pregnant. It was a cock-up.

Roger Kilroy-Silk

Since I met my new girlfriend I can't eat, drink or sleep. I'm broke.

Rick Nelson

At first I thought he was walking a dog. Then I realised it was his date.

Edith Massey

One advantage of being pregnant is that you don't have to worry about getting pregnant.

Peter Nicholls

One night Mr and Mrs Reginald Bingham went to Ciro's. They had been married only about six months. Mr Bingham had never been to Ciro's before in his life. His surprise, therefore, upon seeing his wife there, was considerable.

Ben Travers

I went to a discount massage parlour the other night – it was self-service.

Rodney Dangerfield

I am one of the few males who suffers from penis envy.

Woody Allen

If treated properly sex can be the most beautiful thing in the world.

Elizabeth Taylor

I believe in clubs for women – but only if every other form of persuasion fails.

W.C. Fields

A man always remembers his first love with special tenderness, but after that he begins to bunch them.

H.L. Mencken

All men are mortal. Socrates was mortal. Therefore, all men are Socrates. Which means that all men are homosexuals.

Woody Allen

I look like an elderly wasp in an interesting condition.

Mrs Patrick Campbell

Sex and death, two things that come once in a lifetime. Only after death you're not nauseous.

Woody Allen

PMS means never wanting to say you're sorry.

Diana Jordan

One of the best things about marriage is that it gets young people to bed at a decent hour.

M.M. Musselman

Our union has been blessed with issues.

Peter de Vries

Oh God, in the name of Thine only beloved Son, Jesus Christ, Our Lord, let him phone me now.

Dorothy Parker

My wife told me her waters had just gone so I told her not to worry that I would get her some more.

Dave Barry

A husband is what is left of a lover after the nerve has been extracted.

Helen Rowland

The first time Adam had the chance, he put the blame on a woman.

Nancy Astor

If you let women have their way, you will generally get even with them in the end.

Will Rogers

So far as it is known, no widow has ever eloped.

Edgar W. Howe

I think it's a great idea to talk during sex as long as it's about snooker.

Steve Davis

She was a classy girl – she smoked a fifty-cent cigar.

W.C. Fields

I have got little feet because nothing grows in the shade.

Dolly Parton

Women represent the triumph of matter over mind, just as men represent the triumph of mind over morals.

Oscar Wilde

The happiness of a married man depends on the people he has not married.

Oscar Wilde

Women delight in men over seventy. They offer one the devotion of a lifetime.

Oscar Wilde

If little green men land in your back yard, hide any little green women you've got in the house.

Mike Harding

I used to be with three women until 5 a.m. Now I'm in training, it's five women until 3 a.m.

Alberto Tomba

My wife has helped me considerably with my career. Late one night in 1924 we got home from somewhere and I said I was hungry, so she gave me a verbal picture of the location of the pantry.

Ring Lardner

Men are creatures with two legs and eight hands.

Jayne Mansfield

Hollywood divorces cost so much because they're worth it.

Johnny Carson

A lot of women complain about periods but I don't because I think they're brilliant. Especially if you know somebody who lives next door who you can't stand who's got a white sofa.

Jo Brand

The other night I said to my wife, 'Do you feel that the excitement has gone out of our marriage?' She said, 'I'll discuss it with you during the next commercial'.

Milton Berle

This 'relationship' business is one big waste of time. It is just Mother Nature urging you to breed, breed, breed. Learn from nature. Learn from our friend the spider. Just mate once and then kill him.

Ruby Wax

They buried the hatchet, but in a shallow well marked grave.

Dorothy Walworth

I'd love to go out with you, but my favourite commercial is on TV.

Rita Rudner

I blame myself for my boyfriend's death. I shot him.

Jo Brand

The real drawback to marriage is that it makes one unselfish. And unselfish people are colourless.

Oscar Wilde

She had so many gold teeth she used to have to sleep with her head in a safe.

W.C. Fields

My wife will buy anything marked down. Last week she brought home an escalator.

Henny Youngman

Sometimes a man just can't satisfy all of a woman's desires. Which is why God invented dental floss.

Susanne Kollrack

I sometimes wonder whether all the female nudity you see in newspapers and magazines may not reflect a certain wistfulness for the days when men and women were more easily told apart.

Evelyn Waugh

Among these Mr Quiverful, the rector of Puddingdale, whose wife still continued to present him from year to year with fresh pledges of her love.

Anthony Trollope

Please God, keep me from telephoning him, please God.

Dorothy Parker

Bestiality is a poke in a pig.

Andrew Austin

I've never been married, but I tell people I'm divorced so they won't think something is wrong with me.

Elayne Boosler

To attract men, I wear a perfume called 'new car interior'.

Rita Rudner

I'm looking for Miss Right, or at least Miss Right Now.

Robin Williams

I'd love to go out with you, but I want to spend more time with my blender.

Rita Rudner

My husbands have been very unlucky.

Lucrezia Borgia

Women like silent men. They think they are listening.

Marcel Achard

My girlfriend has the most beautiful breasts in the world: five.

Emo Philips

When you get married you forget about kissing other women.

Pat Boone

You know that look women have when they want sex? Me neither.

Steve Martin

I never knew any woman who could compare with Dolly Lestrange in the art of drawing out and waking into rampant life any spice of the devil which might be lurking latent in a man's soul.

Rhoda Broughton

No wonder that girl was licking David Mellor's toes. She was probably trying to get as far away from his face as possible.

Tommy Docherty

I was in San Francisco when the great earthquake struck, but we were kinda busy in the bedroom and we didn't notice what was going on outside.

John Barrymore

When a man talks dirty to a woman, it's sexual harassment. When a woman talks dirty to a man, it's $3.95 a minute.

Steven Wright

Women will sometimes admit making a mistake. The last man who admitted that he was wrong was General George Custer.

Rita Rudner

One of the principal differences between a woman and a volcano is that a volcano doesn't fake eruptions.

Tim Dedopulos

Dear wife, I acknowledge receipt of your complaint number 387,501.

W.C. Fields

The morning the wife and I broke up you could hear a pin drop in our house. I didn't see the hand grenade in her other hand.

Roy Brown

A man who won't lie to a woman has very little consideration for her feelings.

Olin Miller

It is only man, whose intellect is clouded by his sexual impulses, that could give the name of 'the fairer sex' to that undersized, narrow-shouldered, broad-hipped and short-legged race.

Arthur Schopenhauer

Bridge is not a sex substitute. Sex is a bridge substitute. The partnership is as intimate as marriage.

Helen Knott

She said she would scream for help. I told her I didn't need any help.

Bob Hope

The first man that can think up a good explanation of how he can be in love with his wife and another woman is going to win that prize they're always giving out in Sweden.

Mary Cecil

I wasn't being free with my hands: I was trying to guess her weight.

W. C. Fields

Love is being able to squeeze your lover's spots.

Zoe Ball

There is nothing wrong with pregnancy. Half of the people in the world wouldn't be here today if it wasn't for women being pregnant.

Sarah Kennedy

Whatever you say against women, they are better creatures than men, for men were made of clay, but women were made of man.

Jonathan Swift

A man who says his wife can't take a joke forgets she took him.

John Simpson

During sex my girlfriend always wants to talk to me. Just the other night she called me from a motel.

Rodney Dangerfield

Before getting married, find out if you're really in love. Ask yourself, 'Would I mind getting financially destroyed by this person?'

Johnny Carson

Two is company. Three is fifty bucks.

Joan Rivers

Be careful of men who are bald and rich; the arrogance of 'rich' usually cancels out the niceness of 'bald'.

Rita Rudner

All men make mistakes, but married men find out about them sooner.

Red Skelton

I refuse to take a DNA test to establish if I am the father of an eighteen-year-old beauty queen. I admit I have fathered at least eleven children by five different women, but this case could open the floodgates to dozens of other claims. I might run out of blood.

Joseph Estrada

Anyone who thinks that marriage is a fifty-fifty proposition doesn't understand women or fractions.

Jackie Mason

After seven years of marriage, I'm sure of just two things: first, never wallpaper together, and second, you'll need two bathrooms, both for her.

Dennis Miller

Then I said to her, 'So you're a feminist: how cute'.

Robin Williams

Women do laundry every couple of days. A man will wear every article of clothing he owns, including his surgical pants that were hip about eight years ago, before he will do his laundry. When he is finally out of clothes, he will wear a dirty sweatshirt inside out, rent a U-haul and take his mountain of clothes to the laundromat, and expect to meet a beautiful woman there.

Dave Barry

Three wise men? You must be joking.

Rita Rudner

I never saw two fatter lovers, for she is as big as Murray. Seriously speaking, it is a very good marriage, and acting under the direction of medical men, with perseverance and the use of a stimulating diet, there may be an heir to the house of Henderland.

Sydney Smith

One night I made love from one o'clock to five past two. It was the time they put the clocks forward.

Gary Shandling

Never marry a widow unless her first husband was hanged.

James Kelly

I am the most desirable man in the world. Indeed, if I put my mind to it, I am sure I could pass the supreme test and lure Miss Taylor away from Mr Burton.

Noël Coward

My name is Grace but everyone calls me Gracie for short.

Gracie Allen

Marry me Emily and I'll never look at another horse.

Groucho Marx

Dior's New Look: these are clothes worn by a man who doesn't know women, never had one and dreams of being one.

Coco Chanel

Marriage is natural: like poaching, or drinking or wind in the stummick.

H. G. Wells

When a man's best friend is his dog, that dog has a problem.

Edward Abbey

She was built like a brick chickenhouse.

W. C. Fields

For their twenty-fifth wedding anniversary, they gave each other inscribed tombstones. Hers read 'Here lies my wife, cold as usual' while his read 'Here lies my husband, stiff at last'.

Jack South

Lewis Carroll was as fond of me as he could be of anyone over the age of ten.

Ellen Terry

Personally I don't see why a man can't have a dog and a girl. But if you can afford only one of them, get a dog.

Groucho Marx

I was married by a judge but I should have asked for a jury.

Groucho Marx

Some people think my wife is pretty and others think she's ugly. Me: I think she's pretty ugly.

Les Dawson

We had a lot in common. I loved him and he loved him.

Shelley Winters

Husbands are like fires. They go out when unattended.

Zsa Zsa Gabor

The only woman I have ever loved has left me and finally married: my mother.

Emo Philips

You may marry the man of your dreams, ladies, but fourteen years later you're married to a couch that burps.

Roseanne Barr

I knew right away that Rock Hudson was gay when he did not fall in love with me.

Gina Lollobrigida

To have a happy marriage, tell your spouse everything, except the essentials.

Cynthia Nelms

Both marriage and death ought to be welcome. The one promises happiness, doubtless the other assures it.

Mark Twain

There is, of course, no reason for the existence of the male sex except that sometimes one needs help with moving the piano.

Rebecca West

Nothing in our culture, not even home computers, is more overrated than the epidermal felicity of two featherless bipeds in desperate congress.

Quentin Crisp

Marriage is an outmoded silly convention started by the cavemen and encouraged by the florists and the jewellers.

Olivia de Havilland

A girl phoned me the other day and said, 'Come on over, there's nobody home.' I went over. Nobody was home.

Rodney Dangerfield

Sex is something the children never discuss in the presence of their elders.

Rodney Dangerfield

'Ms' is a syllable which sounds like a bumblebee breaking wind.

Hortense Calisher

It was out of the closet and into the streets for the nation's homosexuals in the 1970s. This didn't do much for the streets but, on the other hand, your average closet has improved immeasurably.

John Weidman

It takes only four men to wallpaper a house, but you have to slice them thinly.

Jo Brand

I didn't get too many women running after me. It was their husbands who'd be after me.

Charlie George

When I was young it was considered immodest for the bride to do anything on the honeymoon except to weep gently and ask for glasses of water.

Noël Coward

Madam, if you wish to have a baby by me, surely you don't mean by unartificial insemination.

James Thurber

I have known couples stay up till three in the morning, each hoping that the other would finally give in and make the bed.

Katharine Hepburn

How many husbands have I had? You mean apart from my own?

Zsa Zsa Gabor

If you want to find out some things about yourself – and in vivid detail too - just try calling your wife fat.

P.J. O'Rourke

Stan Waltz has decided to take unto himself a wife but he hasn't decided whose yet.

Peter de Vries

Men don't shop even for their own underpants.

Germaine Greer

I don't worry about terrorism. I was married for two years.

Sam Kinison

Two cures for love:
1. Don't see him. Don't phone or write a letter.
2. The easy way: get to know him better.

Wendy Cope

Marilyn Monroe and Joe Demaggio have divorced. It just goes to show that no man can be expert at our two national pastimes.

Joe E. Brown

Men are always better at offering women things that men like: a man will give his wife a pair of fishing boots in his size.

Katharine Whitehorn

Don't you realise that as long as you have to sit down to pee, you'll never be a dominant force in the world? You'll never be a convincing technocrat or middle manager. Because people will know. She's in there sitting down.

Don DeLillo

One thing men can do better than women is read a road map. Men read maps better because only a male mind could conceive of an inch equalling a hundred miles.

Roseanne Barr

The trouble with men is that there are not enough of them.

Hermione Gingold

She was the original good time that was had by all.

Bette Davis

A sure sign a man is going to be unfaithful is if he has a penis.

Jo Brand

Sex at ninety-three is like playing snooker with a rope.

George Burns

I'm always attracted to the wrong kind of guy: like the Pope.

Carol Leifer

I read recently that love is entirely a matter of chemistry. That must be why my wife treats me like toxic waste.

David Bissonette

Whatever you may look like, marry a man of your own age: as your beauty fades, so will his eyesight.

Phyllis Diller

'Duck behind the sofa,' she told me. 'There's no duck behind the sofa,' I told her.

Groucho Marx

We were fast and furious: I was fast and she was furious.

Max Kaufmann

Is that a gun in your pocket, or are you just pleased to see me?

Mae West

Commitment is what every woman wants; men can't even spell it.

Laura Zigman

The high-heeled shoe is a marvellously contradictory item; it brings a woman to a man's height but makes sure she cannot keep up with him.

Germaine Greer

Marriage is very difficult. Very few of us are fortunate enough to marry multimillionaire girls with thirty-nine-inch busts who have undergone frontal lobotomies.

Tony Curtis

If I never see that woman again, it's too soon.

Groucho Marx

At every party there are two kinds of people: those who want to go home and those who don't. The trouble is they are usually married to each other.

Ann Landers

No two women are alike, in fact no one woman is alike.

Alfred Austin

My wife and I were married in a toilet: it was a marriage of convenience.

Tommy Cooper

My wife and I have enjoyed over forty years of wedded blitz.

Hugh Leonard

Men get such brilliant ideas during sex because they are plugged into a genius.

Mary Lynch

How do you know if it's time to wash the dishes and clean your house? Look inside your pants. If you find a penis in there, it's not time.

Jo Brand

Fighting is essentially a masculine idea; a woman's weapon is her tongue.

Hermione Gingold

Never trust a woman who wears mauve, whatever her age may be, or a woman over thirty-five who is fond of pink ribbons. It always means they have a history.

Oscar Wilde

Marriage is a triumph of habit over hate.

Oscar Levant

I walked into that wedding with both eyes shut. Her brother shut one and her father shut the other.

Billy Bennett

I have learned that only two things are necessary to keep one's wife happy. First, let her think she's having her own way. And second, let her have it.

Lyndon B. Johnson

I am sorry to say that the generality of women who have excelled in wit have failed in chastity.

Elizabeth Montagu

I live by a man's code, designed to fit a man's world, yet at the same time I never forgot that a woman's first job is to choose the right shade of lipstick.

Carole Lombard

It is when your boyfriend asks you to accompany him on a river trip, at night, in the boat he has built at evening classes that a crisis comes. There is no tactful way to tell a man he has a leaky vessel.

Grace Bradbury

The word androgyny is misbegotten: conveying something like John Travolta and Farrah Fawcett-Majors Scotch-taped together.

Mary Daly

If you have been married more than ten years, being good in bed means you don't steal the covers.

Brenda Davidson

I saw on television the other day some men who like to dress up as women and when they do they can no longer parallel park.

Roseanne Barr

Do you realise that Eve was the only woman who ever took a man's side?

Milton Berle

Women do not find it difficult nowadays to behave like men, but they often find it extremely difficult to behave like gentlemen.

Compton Mackenzie

A wife can often surprise her husband on their wedding anniversary by merely mentioning it.

E. C. McKenzie

My sister gives me the creeps: all her old boyfriends.

Terri Kelly

I think the only good thing to be said about leotards is that they're a very effective deterrent against any sort of unwanted sexual attention. If you're wearing stretch knickers, and stretch tights, and a stretch Lycra leotard, you might as well try and sexually harass a trampoline.

Victoria Wood

I am tired of being a free finishing school for men.

Suzanne Wolstenholme

One special form of contact which consists of mutual approximation of the mucous membranes of the lips in a kiss has received a sexual value among the civilised nations, though the parts of the body do not belong to the sexual apparatus and merely form the entrance to the digestive tract.

Sigmund Freud

My husband and I didn't sign a pre-nuptial agreement. We signed a mutual suicide pact.

Roseanne Barr

Do we have impotent men in here tonight? Oh, I see, you can't get your arms up either.

Roseanne Barr

Woman is fickle. Giver her a tickle.

Ken Dodd

Rule One: The sun will rise in the East. Rule Two: As long as there are rich men trying not to feel old, there will be young girls trying not to feel poor.

Julie Burchill

If I did not wear torn pants, orthopaedic shoes, frantic dishevelled hair, that is to say, if I did not tone down my beauty, people would go mad. Married men would run amuck.

Brenda Ueland

Kathy Sue Loudermilk was a lovely child and a legend before her sixteenth birthday. She was twenty-one, however, before she knew an automobile had a front seat.

Lewis Grizzard

Women are most fascinating between the ages of thirty-five and forty, after they have won a few races and know how to pace themselves. Since few women ever pass forty, maximum fascination can continue indefinitely.

Christian Dior

Most married couples, even though they love each other very much in theory, tend to view each other in practice as large teeming flaw colonies, the result being that they get on each other's nerves and regularly erupt into vicious emotional shouting matches over such issues as toaster settings.

Dave Barry

Women have simple tastes. They can get pleasure out of the conversation of children in arms and men in love.

H.L. Mencken

I hate the sound of an ambulance. My first wife ran away with an ambulance driver and every time I hear a siren, I get the shakes thinking he might be bringing her back.

Jackie Martling

When women go wrong, men go right after them.

Mae West

Alan Clark is not sixty-five going on sixteen. He is sixty-five going on twelve.

Jane Clark

She was about six feet tall and had a bosom as shapeless as a plate of scrambled eggs.

Richard Gordon

Dolly Parton has a yacht in Seattle and it's windy there. One day she hung her bra to dry and woke up in Brazil.

Phyllis Diller

I bought my wife a sex manual but half the pages were missing. We went straight from foreplay to post-natal depression.

Bob Monkhouse

My girlfriend was so big she could breastfeed Watford.

Brian Conley

Most husbands remember where and when they got married. What stumps them is why.

E.C. McKenzie

Before we got married, my wife was my secretary, now she's my treasurer.

Bob Goddard

In olden times, sacrifices were made at the altar, a custom which is still continued.

Helen Rowland

If you want to stay single, look for the perfect woman.

Ken Alstad

She was a pretty nice guy: for a girl.

Robert Mitchum

Women don't gamble as much as men because their total instinct for gambling is satisfied by marriage.

Gloria Steinem

My girlfriend has to have a kidney transplant but I'm not worried about her because she hasn't rejected an organ for over twenty years. Seriously though, she could count all the lovers she's had on one hand: if she's holding a calculator.

Tom Cotter

If you ask your husband if he still loves you he will answer, 'I'm still married to you, aren't I?'

Brenda Davidson

I got married again last year because my first wife died in a wishing well.

Tony Gerrard

When you hit seventy you sleep sounder, you feel more alive than when you were thirty. Obviously it's healthier to have women on your mind than on your knees.

Maurice Chevalier

Women have more imagination than men. They need it to tell us how wonderful we are.

Arnold Glasow

If you ask for a doggy bag on a date, you might as well wrap up your genitals too, because you're not going to be needing them for a long time.

Jerry Seinfeld

When my husband complained to me that he couldn't remember when we last had sex I said, 'Well I can, and that's why we ain't doing it'.

Roseanne Barr

My wife and I are inseparable. Sometimes it takes four people to pull us apart.

Milton Berle

When I lived with a homosexual photographer, it was so nice to relax with that kind of man, to enjoy his delightful malicious wit and intelligence, without having to worry about bruising his male ego, his machismo, and having to deal with all that ritualised wrestling at the end of an otherwise cheerful evening.

Katherine Anne Porter

I know so much about men because I went to night school.

Mae West

A woman seeking a husband is the most unscrupulous of all beasts of prey.

George Bernard Shaw

When a woman says she wants to go out and get a job to express herself, it usually means she is hopelessly behind in the ironing.

Oliver Reed

On some of the Pacific Islands there were so few women that the guys in the forces would start howling at the sight of two coconuts close together.

Bob Hope

Being a woman is a terribly difficult trade, since it consists principally of dealing with men.

Joseph Conrad

My ex-wife Joan Collins is a commodity who would sell her own bowel movements.

Anthony Newley

I didn't suspect it was an orgy until three days later.

S.J. Perelman

There are rumours floating around that I am a lesbian, which I assume were started by men who were really jealous that I was such a looker yet so unattainable.

Jo Brand

The difference between my wife and a terrorist is that you can negotiate with a terrorist.

Frank Carson

I love to shop after a bad relationship. I buy a new outfit and it makes me feel better. Sometimes, when I see a really great outfit, I'll break up with someone on purpose.

Rita Rudner

On our honeymoon my husband told me to unbutton my pyjamas, and I wasn't wearing any.

Phyllis Diller

Anything worth doing well is worth doing slowly.

Gypsy Rose Lee

Since I've been married I don't have to worry about bad breath. I never get a chance to open my mouth.

Rodney Dangerfield

Never work for a man shorter than yourself and never break wind while making love. These are the only immutable laws in life.

Richard Girling

A faithful woman is one who doesn't want two men to suffer at the same time.

Jan Vercammer

My wife and I thought we were in love but it turned out to be benign.

Woody Allen

A toy company announced it is coming out with a brand-new virtual pet that eats, sleeps, burps and passes wind. It is designed to show young women what it's like to be married.

Conan O'Brien

The trouble with men and urinals is that men aren't demanding enough. If they hit something, they're happy.

Rita Rudner

Husbands think we should know where everything is: like the uterus is the tracking device. He asks me, 'Roseanne, do we have any cheetos left?' Like he can't go over to the sofa and lift it himself.

Roseanne Barr

A caring husband is a man so interested in his wife's happiness that he will hire a detective to find out who is responsible for it.

Milton Berle

The greatest tragedy is to marry a man for love and then find out he has no money.

Zsa Zsa Gabor

Philandering with a married woman is the most exaggerated form of amusement that has ever been invented.

Somerset Maugham

When a man sends flowers it is a sign that he admires more women than one.

Somerset Maugham

A journalist once asked me if I had ever slept with a woman. I replied that I had been accused of being many things in my life but never of being a lesbian.

Michael MacLiammoir

If there is anybody out there who has just bought the book *The Joy of Sex*, there is a misprint on page 206.

Phyllis Diller

I don't mind my wife having the last word. In fact I'm delighted when she reaches it.

Walter Matthau

It was not a bosom to repose upon, but it was a capital bosom to hang jewels on.

Charles Dickens

I like you so much that sometimes it's an effort to remember that you're a woman at all.

Terence Rattigan

Ernest Hemingway's effect upon women is such that they want to go right out and get him and bring him home stuffed.

Dorothy Parker

I've had so many men, the FBI come to me for fingerprints.

Mae West

My wife gives very good headache.

Rodney Dangerfield

My advice to girls is first, don't smoke – to excess; second, don't drink – to excess; third, don't marry – to excess.

Mark Twain

Only time can heal a broken heart, just as only time can heal his broken arms and legs.

Miss Piggy

The closest I ever came to a *menage à trois* was once when I dated a schizophrenic.

Rita Rudner

The women's movement would probably be more successful if men were running it.

Jimmy Williams

Whenever you apologise to your wife the answer is always the same – 'It's too late now and it's the wrong kind of apology'.

Dave Barry

I dated this girl for two years and then the nagging started – 'Tell me your name, tell me your name'.

Mike Binder

The sock is a highly sensitive conjugal object.

Jean-Claude Kaufman

If Jack Lemmon was a homosexual, I'd marry him.

Walter Matthau

A man is simply a woman's way of making another woman.

Samuel Butler

When I said I had sex for seven hours, that included dinner and a movie.

Phil Collins

I'm not offended by all the dumb-blonde jokes because I know I'm not dumb. I also know I'm not blonde.

Dolly Parton

A man without a woman is like a neck without a pain.

W.C. Fields

Catherine Deneuve is the man I would have liked to be.

Gerard Depardieu

Men don't understand washing machine controls because they are written in woman.

Jeremy Clarkson

I don't think my wife likes me very much. When I had a heart attack she wrote for an ambulance.

Frank Carson

I love being married. I was single for a long time and I just got sick of finishing my own sentences.

Brian Kiley

What makes sex so popular is that you don't have to get dressed up for it.

George Burns

I reckon it is easier to shoot your wife than to have to shoot a different man every week.

Dick Hills

I have a mirrored ceiling over my bed because I like to know what I am doing.

Mae West

O, she is the antidote to desire.

William Congreve

Men are hunters. Women are just bargain hunters.

Deirdre O'Kane

Greta Garbo was every man's harmless fantasy mistress. She gave you the impression that, if your imagination had to sin, it could at least congratulate itself on its impeccable taste.

Alistair Cooke

You can tell it's love, the real thing, when you dream of slitting his throat.

Wendy Cope

Every night when the moon is full a werewolf turns into a wolf – him and thirty million other guys.

Lou Costello

Most men in this town think monogamy is some kind of wood.

Mike Werb

I have chosen a very plain girlfriend – buggers can't be choosers.

Maurice Bowra

He asked me if I wanted to go back to his place. I told him I didn't know if two people could fit under a rock.

Rita Rudner

Playboy has just produced a new magazine for married men. It has the same pictures month after month after month.

Lisa Clark

I know that blokes have feelings too – but who cares?

Jo Brand

New lovers should have a minimum isolation period of say, six months, so as not to nauseate everyone they meet.

Kathy Lette

A psychiatrist told me and my wife that we should have sex every night – now we never see each other.

Rodney Dangerfield

You get to go through 36 hours of contractions; he gets to hold your hand and say 'focus, breathe, push'.

Joan Rivers

What's wrong with you men? Would hair stop growing on your chests if you asked directions somewhere?

Erma Bombeck

If your girlfriend wants to leave you, she should give you two weeks' notice, there should be severance pay, and before they leave, they should have to find you a temp.

Bob Ettinger

Men who have fought in the world's bloodiest wars are apt to faint at the sight of a truly foul diaper.

Gary Christenson

To intimidate your daughter's date when he picks her up, let him see you sprinkling some dust on her before she leaves. Say: 'It makes fingerprinting easier.'

Mike McQueen

I think, therefore I am single.

Liz Winstead

In lovemaking, what my ex-husband lacked in size, he made up for in speed.

Roseanne Barr

The two times they pronounce you anything in life are when you are man and wife or when they pronounce you dead on arrival.

Dennis Miller

Marriage is the only legal form of pickpocketing.

Alice Kahn

Here's a bit of advice for office managers – keep the sexual harassment complaint forms in the bottom drawer so you'll get a great view of the secretary's butt as she gets one out.

Denis Leary

The difference between a man and a municipal bond is that municipal bonds eventually mature.

Agnes Langer

Heidi Abromowitz has had more hands up her dress than the Muppets.

Joan Rivers

I don't think it's a big deal that swans mate for life. If you're a swan, you're probably not going to find a swan that looks much better than the one you've got, so why not mate for life?

Jack Handey

There ain't nothin' an ol' man can do but bring me a message from a young one.

Moms Mabley

I'm getting old. When I squeeze into a tight parking space, I'm sexually satisfied for the day.

Rodney Dangerfield

If he asks: 'Your place or mine?' say, 'Both. You go to your place and I'll go to mine'.

Bette Midler

I have known and respected your husband for many years and what is good enough for him is good enough for me.

Groucho Marx

In the last stage of labour I threatened to take my husband to court for concealing a lethal weapon in his boxer shorts.

Linda Fiterman

If you love someone, set them free. If they come back, they're probably broke.

Rhonda Dickson

Women should not be enlightened or educated in any way. They should, in fact, be segregated as they are the cause of hideous and involuntary erections in holy men.

St. Augustine

A control freak is any man who behaves like a woman and a nymphomaniac is any woman who behaves like a man.

Patrick Murray

I'm looking for a perfume to overpower men – I'm sick of karate.

Phyllis Diller

My Uncle Harry was an early feminist. At a race meeting in Ayr, he threw himself under a suffragette.

Arnold Brown

It is not good enough to spend time and ink in describing the penultimate sensations and physical movements of people getting into a state of rut; we all know them too well.

John Galsworthy

Lo, an intelligent opinion in the mouth of a woman horrifieth a man even as the scissors in the mouth of a babe.

Helen Rowland

Men wake up as good-looking as they went to bed. Women somehow deteriorate during the night.

Jerry Seinfeld

The only really firm rule of taste about cross-dressing is that neither sex should ever wear anything they haven't figured out how to go to the bathroom in.

P. J. O'Rourke

In a world without men, there would be no war – just intense negotiations every twenty-eight days.

Robin Williams

It is my observation that women who complain of sexual harassment are, more often than not, revoltingly ugly.

Auberon Waugh

Women who insist upon having the same options as men would do well to consider the option of being the strong silent type.

Fran Lebowitz

Men are better than cats because men pee only on the carpet in the loo.

Jo Brand

My wife thinks I should buy her a new dress just because she's fed up of treading on the veil of the one she's got.

Roy Brown

The difference between a man and a battery is that a battery has a plus side.

Jo Brand

Women are like banks, boy, breaking and entering is a serious business.

Joe Orton

Monogamy is the Western custom of one wife and hardly any mistresses.

Saki

God, why didn't you make women first – when you were fresh?

Yves Montand

In a lonely hearts advert, 'good-looking' means he's an arrogant bastard, 'huggable' means he's overweight and has got more hair than a yeti.

Mary Gold

A gold rush is what happens when a line of chorus girls spots a man with a bank roll.

Mae West

The first divorce is the hardest. After that you know the routine.

Elizabeth Taylor

I am never troubled by sexual desires. In fact I rather enjoy them.

Tommy Cooper

Mme de Genlis, in order to avoid the scandal of coquetry, always yielded easily.

Charles de Talleyrand

A newly-wed is a guy who tells his wife when he gets a pay raise.

Leonard Levinson

If your home burns down, rescue the dogs. At least they'll be faithful to you.

Lee Marvin

It takes a lot of experience for a girl to kiss like a beginner.

Dorothy Parker

My advice is to keep two mistresses. Few men have the stamina for more.

Ovid

Sex is a subject like any other subject. Every bit as interesting as agriculture.

Muriel Spark

As a couple, they were a perfect illustration of the equation zero plus zero equals zero.

Patrick Murray

A woman is someone who can remember a hat she bought in 1938 but cannot remember what is trumps.

Joseph Soaper

My ideal man is young and handsome and looks as if his teeth will stay in all night.

Victoria Wood

Being a woman must be a great thing or otherwise so many men wouldn't be wanting to do it.

Gilda Radner

I will not meet you at the pier, my love, as it will probably be chilly.

Anton Chekhov

We ask women to do only two things – menstruate and have babies, and look at the fuss they make about both.

Scott McClue

Of course I've known for years our marriage has been a mockery. My body lying there night after night in the wasted moonlight. I know now how the Taj Mahal must feel.

Alan Bennett

Charles de Talleyrand is in love with himself and he doesn't have a rival on earth.

Napoleon Bonaparte

A wife is a person who can look in a drawer and find her husband's socks that aren't there.

Dan Bennett

So long as spiders continue to invade our home, I can rest secure in the knowledge she daren't divorce me.

Gerry Hanson

Women give men the very gold in their lives. But they invariably want it back in small change.

Oscar Wilde

I like a man with an open chequebook sort of face.

Joan Rivers

A ventriloquist's dummy always seems to have a very active social and sexual life. He's always talking about dates and women that he knows and bringing them back to his suitcase at night.

Jerry Seinfeld

Sure I'll tie the marital knot – as long as it's around her neck.

W.C. Fields

God created lesbians so that feminists can't breed.

Roy Brown

The secret of a happy marriage remains a secret.

Henny Youngman

Women over fifty cannot have babies because they would put them down and forget where they left them.

Oliver Reed

This lovely young girl said to me the other day, 'Hello, handsome, could you tell me the way to the optician's?'

Ken Dodd

A guy who would cheat on his wife would cheat at cards.

Texas Guinan

Greatest horror – I dream I am married and wake up shrieking.

J.M. Barrie

I was devastated to pick up a newspaper the other

day and read that eighty-two per cent of British men would rather sleep with a goat than with me.

Sarah Ferguson

I don't care what they say, women make the best wives.

Chic Young

The closest I've ever come to saying 'no' is 'not now, we're landing'.

Ted Danson

On the one hand, men never experience childbirth. On the other hand, we can open all our own jars.

Bruce Willis

Are all the men in your social circle either spoken for or unspeakable?

Suzi Godson

Women may be able to fake orgasms, but men can fake whole relationships.

Sharon Stone

Of course, darling, return the ring – but keep the diamonds.

Zsa Zsa Gabor

My wife says I never listen to her. At least that's what I think she said.

Milton Berle

I discovered my wife in bed with another man and I was crushed. So I said, 'Get off me you two'.

Emo Philips

Sex is a good thing. Someday I hope to do it again.

Jerry Seinfeld

I wanted to have a prenuptial agreement – not to get married.

Anne MacHale

One thing I don't understand about women - why do they have to have colour-coordinated underwear?

Robin Williams

There will always be a battle between the sexes because men and women want different things – men want women and women want men.

George Burns

My sleeping wife was snoring with all the refinement of a bronchial warthog. She sounded like the death rattle of a moose with piles.

Les Dawson

I never kept any secrets from my wife – mind you I tried.

Mitch Murray

Fall not in love – it will stick to your face.

Dan Ackroyd

On my second honeymoon I sent a telegram to my friends saying "Nothing new to report".

Carole Lombard

They call it a 'Pearl Wedding' because after thirty years together, you feel like stringing yourself up.

Don MacLean

One of the first signs that your wife is unhappy is when she starts lining the budgie's cage with your wedding pictures.

Roy Brown

Never do anything in bed that you can't pronounce.

Mitch Murray

Nothing confuses a man more than driving behind a woman who does everything right.

Henny Youngman

If you haven't seen a man and he hasn't called in about three weeks and if you are in doubt about his whereabouts, the chances are he is not in an emergency room moaning your name.

Diane Conway

If a 22-year-old toy boy came up to me, expressing his undying love, I would suspect his mental health.

Phyllis Diller

Now it's men who can't commit and you find forty-five-year-old men saying they're not ready for marriage. No, you're not, you're ready for death.

Joan Rivers

When can one love someone truly? Only when one is safely married – and then with the greatest discretion.

Oscar Wilde

I met this drop-dead gorgeous girl at a party. I said: 'You're gorgeous' She said: 'Drop dead'.

Mitch Murray

I am the world's most married woman. I'm now ready to get married again – it will be marriage number 23 and it's going to last for ever. All my ex-husbands are friends with one another and I am friends with all of them.

Linda Evans

Never cry over a man. Just yell 'next'.

Denise Gilbert

I met my wife at a singles bar. We were both very surprised.

Brian Conley

How can I describe her looks? Can you imagine Yasser Arafat with plaits?

Mitch Murray

A dating agency – it's like a good bowel movement; there is an immediate elimination.

Susan Powter

Married life ain't so bad after you get so you can eat the things your wife likes.

Kin Hubbard

Never go out with an old man. I went out with an old man one night – he gave me a love bite and left his teeth in my neck.

Joan Rivers

My wife and I have a great way of settling arguments – I admit I'm wrong and she admits she's right.

Jack Benny

Everything my wife and I do is on a 50-50 basis – I tell her what to do and she tells me where to go.

Mitch Murray

I don't give women a second thought because the first one covers everything.

Henny Youngman

We have women in the military but they don't put us in the front lines. They don't know if we can fight or if we can kill. I think we can. All the general has to do is walk over to the women and say:

'You see the enemy over there? They say you look fat in those uniforms'.

Elayne Boosler

As a seventy-five-year-old widower, I do find it off-putting when the opposite sex stresses 'own teeth and hair essential'. I would never dream of using anyone else's.

Alfred Norris

I was oversexed for only once in my life – from 1914 to 1981.

George Burns

Remember, marriage is a two-way street. I don't know what that means, but remember it.

George Burns

All honeymooners should hire a third party to ease the conversation during that most difficult time.

Robert Morley

The material for my book, *A Guide to Men,* was collected directly from nature at great personal risk by the author.

Helen Rowland

My wife was afraid of the dark. Then she saw me naked and now she's afraid of the light.

Rodney Dangerfield

A man's heart may have a secret sanctuary where only one woman may enter, but it is full of little anterooms which are seldom vacant.

Helen Rowland

Marriage is a wonderful institution. If it weren't for marriage, husbands and wives would have to fight with total strangers.

Patrick Murray

He took his misfortune like a man – he blamed it on his wife.

Bob Phillips

For novelty in your sex life, both partners should sit in the cupboard under the stairs and try to identify parts of the gas meter and vacuum cleaner by touch.

Mark Leigh

If there were no husbands, who would look after our mistresses?

George Moore

It is better to have loved even your wife than never to have loved at all.

Edgar Saltus

You must have women dressed, if it is only for the pleasure of imagining them as Venuses.

George Moore

It's our story exactly! He bold as a hawk, she soft as the dawn.

James Thurber

Every decision a woman makes is right.

Germaine Greer

Love is a painful but not a dignified malady, I think, like piles.

Cyril Connolly

My recipe for marital happiness is whenever you can, read at meals.

Cyril Connolly

People ask me what my favourite colour is – I'd say blue. But you certainly wouldn't want a girl to be that colour after a bout of lovemaking. Who needs that again?

Emo Philips

Oh, yes, I've tried my hand at sex.

Emo Philips

I never speak of my ex-husbands except under hypnosis.

Joan Collins

Hell hath no fury like an ex-wife run to fat.

Tony Parsons

You can tell that a marriage is on the rocks when a couple speak to each other rationally.

Leo Tolstoy

It doesn't matter how often a couple have sex as long as it is the same number for both of them.

Marian Mills

My girlfriend and I almost didn't have the second

date because on the first date I didn't open the car door for her. I just swam to the surface.

Emo Philips

Men who claw their way to the top don't get chastised for it. But look at the grief they gave Joan Rivers for clawing her way to the middle.

Ruth Batchelor

Radical feminists don't want an all-female society. Who would do the washing up for us?

Mandy Young

Sir Christopher Dilke kept his wife in one part of a very big bed and his mistress in another, and neither knew the other was there.

Tony O'Reilly

Glamour is that indefinable something about a girl with a big bosom.

Abe Burrows

The only way a woman can ever reform a man is by boring him so completely that he loses all possible interest in life.

Oscar Wilde

With my bum size, décolletage is my only hope.
The theory is that men will be so mesmerised by
my cleavage that they won't notice my bum.

Jane Owen

My wife is in league with the Devil. I don't know
how much he pays her.

Emo Philips

Even Moses couldn't part her knees.

Joan Rivers

Asking me if I am homosexual or heterosexual is
like asking a man crawling across the Sahara Desert
if he would prefer Malvern or Perrier water.

Alan Bennett

My prescription for writer's block? Alimony – the
world's greatest muse.

Dick Schaap

Being loved can never be a patch on being
murdered. That's when someone really gives their all
for you.

Quentin Crisp

After Oxford, Larkin's homosexual feelings evaporated and were henceforth seemingly confined to his choice of socks.

Andrew Motion

I have been intimate with the bride for many years and I can tell you that a finer woman never walked the streets.

Greville Janner

Intuition is the strange instinct that tells a woman she is right, whether she is or not.

Oscar Wilde

If men liked shopping, they would call it research.

Cynthia Nelms

Sex in marriage is like medicine. Three times a day for the first week. Then once a day for another week. Then once every three or four days until the condition clears up.

Peter de Vries

Speaking of rapists, even the most diehard feminist must admit that's one thing men do better than women.

Gabrielle Burton

My wife and I keep fighting about sex and money.
I think she charges me too much, you know.

Rodney Dangerfield

We've been trying to have a kid. Well, she was
trying. I just lay there.

Bob Saget

Marriage is not a man's idea. A woman must have
thought of it. 'Let me get this straight, honey. I can't
sleep with anyone else for the rest of my life, and if
things don't work out, you get to keep half of my
stuff? What a great idea'.

Bobby Shayton

'Happy marriage' is a contradiction in terms, like
'young poet'.

Philip Larkin

Lawrence was not in the slightest bit queer – later
in life, possibly; even then he had Nancy Astor on
the back of his motorbike.

Lowell Thomas

The old theory was: 'Marry an older man because

they're more mature'. But the new theory is: 'Men don't mature. Marry a younger one'.

Rita Rudner

Marriage is like death. It may be inevitable, but you don't want anyone to start talking dates.

David Chater

I used to be a homosexual, but I had to give it up because it made my eyes water.

Michael Gambon

Marriage is a very good thing, but it's a mistake to make a habit of it.

Somerset Maugham

You can always surprise your husband on your anniversary by just mentioning it.

Al Schlock

What the hell is wrong with forty-year-old women? If our brains were a toy, the box would read 'batteries not included'.

Kathy Lette

To keep your marriage brimming,
With love in the loving cup,
Whenever you're wrong admit it,
Whenever you're right, shut up.

Ogden Nash

Apparently men rarely dream about getting
married. Women have a magazine called *Bride*, but
there's no magazine called *Groom*.

Mary Reinholz

Brevity is the soul of lingerie.

Dorothy Parker

I learned about sex the hard way – from books.

Emo Philips

After making love I said, 'Was it good for you too?'
She said, 'I don't think it was good for anybody'.

Gary Shandling

Save a boyfriend for a rainy day, and another in case
it doesn't rain.

Mae West

I have had the ashes of my late husband Dustin sewn into my breast implants so he will always be close to my heart.

Sandi Canesco

Naomi Jacob's bold adoption of the male persona was so successful that when Paul Bailey himself served her in Harrod's bookshop he mistook her for J.B. Priestley.

Michael Arditti

If brevity is the soul of wit, his penis was a riot.

Mae West

My wife was too beautiful for words, but not for arguments.

John Barrymore

Although Australian men don't go in much for 'foreplay', I never give my wife one without first asking if she's awake.

Les Patterson

I'm into bondage, I like to tie up my wife, gag her and go and watch a football game on TV.

Tom Arnold

Send some flowers to the woman you love and while you're at it, send some to the wife aswell.

Gordon Irving

At seventy-eight, my favourite slow sex position is called 'The Plumber'. You stay in all day, but nobody comes.

John Mortimer

I don't believe in divorce. I believe in widowhood.

Carolyn Green

If diamonds are a girl's best friend and dogs are a man's, which sex is the dumber?

Rita Rudner

A man needs a mistress just to break the monogamy.

Robert Orben

In sex, nothing improves with age.

Steve Martin

Without lying there would be no sex.

Jerry Seinfeld

When my wife complained that I never told her I loved her, I said, 'I told you I loved you when we got married and if I ever change my mind, I'll let you know'.

Liam O'Reilly

When I'm in a wig I'm pretty attractive. I stare at myself in mirrors because I'm my type.

Kevin McDonald

We've split up because the domestic violence got out of hand. I didn't fancy him with all the bruises.

Jackie Clune

Sex in the sixties is great, but it improves if you pull over to the side of the road.

Johnny Carson

This girl says to me, 'Do you want to double up?' I said, 'Sure,' so she kicks me in the groin.

Emo Philips

I had her in my bed gasping for breath and calling out my name. Obviously I didn't hold the pillow down long enough.

Emo Philips

Sex will outlive us all.

Samuel Goldwyn

The first thing I do when I wake up in the morning is to breathe on a mirror and hope it fogs.

Earl Wynn

Never trust anybody who says 'trust me'. Except just this once, of course.

John Varley

When I came into my hotel room last night I found a strange blonde in my bed. I gave her exactly twenty-four hours to get out.

Groucho Marx

Father Christmas advertisements must now be open to both male and female applicants. However, a female appointee must have whiskers, a deep voice, a big belly and a clearly discernible bosom. Children would be terrified of such a woman.

Simon de Bruxelles

Before accepting a marriage proposal take a good

look at his father. If he's still handsome, witty and has all his teeth – marry his father instead.

Diana Jordan

Frenchmen hardly ever speak about their wives: they are afraid to do so in front of people who may know them better than they do.

Charles de Montesquieu

I wouldn't be marrying for the fifth time if it wasn't for keeps.

Joan Collins

Never ask a woman why she's angry at you. She will either get angrier at you for not knowing, or she'll tell you. Both ways, you lose.

Ian Scholes

I've been married seven times. I know nothing about marriage, but a lot about separation.

Artie Shaw

Every woman should learn to fake orgasms – it's just common courtesy.

Joan Rivers

I bought a book called *A Hundred French Mating Positions*, but I never got past page one. I really hate chess.

Emo Philips

Friendship is more tragic than love. It lasts longer.

Oscar Wilde

Marriage is a ceremony in which rings are put on the finger of the lady and through the nose of the gentleman.

Herbert Spencer

Such is the Pastun obsession with sodomy – locals will tell you that birds fly over the city using only one wing, the other covering their posterior.

Tim Reid

Eye contact is a method utilised by a single woman to communicate to a man that she is interested in him. Many women find it difficult to look a man directly in the eyes, not because of shyness, but because a woman's eyes are not located in her chest.

Rita Rudner

Anniversaries are like toilets – men usually manage to miss them.

Jo Brand

There was a girl knocking on my hotel room door all night last night. I finally had to let her out of my room.

Henny Youngman

How marriage ruins a man! It's as demoralising as cigarettes, and far more expensive.

Oscar Wilde

Honey, anything I said seven or eight months ago is inadmissible in an argument. All comments become null and void after twenty-four hours.

Denis Leary

The way to girl's stomach is through her heart.

Philip Schwab

When God created two sexes, He may have been overdoing it.

Charles Smith

I've learned that you cannot make someone love you. All you can do is stalk them and hope they panic and give in.

Emo Philips

My daughter thinks I'm nosy. At least that's what she says in her diary.

Sally Joplin

Apparently man can be cured of drugs, drink, gambling, biting his nails and picking his nose, but not of marrying.

William Faulkner

Woman's first duty is to her dressmaker. What her second duty is no one has yet discovered.

Oscar Wilde

Some warning signs that your lover is getting bored are passionless kisses, frequent sighing and 'moved, left no forwarding address'.

Matt Groening

Remember when I told you I didn't love you no more? Well, I lied.

Robert Cray

I knew absolutely nothing about bondage. I'd always presumed it was just an inventive way of keeping your partner from going home.

Kathy Lette

I have often wanted to drown my troubles, but I can't get my wife to go swimming.

Roy Brown

There is only one thing that keeps me from being happily married – my wife.

Henny Youngman

One reason people get divorced is that they run out of gift ideas.

Robert Byrne

Commitment is different in males and females. In females it is a desire to get married and raise a family. In males it means not picking up other women while out with one's girlfriend.

Rita Rudner

Spencer was searching for a woman interested in gold, inorganic chemistry, outdoor sex and the music of Bach. In short, he was looking for himself, only female.

Woody Allen

Madonna has beautiful skin. You can tell she isn't a scrubber.

Bernard Manning

Even if you could understand women, you still wouldn't believe it.

Frank Dane

Have you ever noticed how so many women's problems are due to men? For example, menstruation, menopause, guynaecology, himorrhoids, mental breakdown?

Joan Rivers

Don't fight over me boys, there's plenty to go around.

Mae West

If you offer help to a woman, you're patronising. If you don't, you're a pig.

Donna McPhail

As a rule women would like to devote as much time to foreplay and the sex act as men would like

to devote to foreplay, the sex act and building a garage.

Dave Barry

The telephone is an invention of the Devil, which abrogates some of the advantages of making a disagreeable person keep his distance.

Ambrose Bierce

Gentlemen prefer blondes but take what they can get.

Don Herold

I am giving up marriage for Lent.

Brian Behan

I thought of him and the love bites on his mirror.

Kathy Lette

Sometimes a man just cannot satisfy all of a woman's desires. Which is why God invented dental floss.

Susanne Kollrack

Women and cats will do just as they please, so men and dogs should get used to the idea.

Robert Heinlein

If a couple walks along like the man was arrested, they're married.

Kin Hubbard

I often hear affectionate husbands call their wives 'My duck'. I wonder if this is a sly allusion to their big bills?

Josh Billings

If we did get a divorce, the only way my husband would find out about it is if they announced it on *Wide World of Sports*.

Joyce Brothers

I married my husband out of spite. I had been let down twice and I decided the next man who asked me would get it.

Daisy Attridge

The trouble about finding a husband for one's mistress is that no other man seems quite good enough.

William Cooper

A lot of guys think the larger a woman's breasts are, the less intelligent she is. I think the larger a woman's breasts are the less intelligent men become.

Anita Wise

A male gets very, very frustrated sitting in a chair all the time because males are biologically driven to go out and hunt giraffes.

Newt Gingrich

What do I know about sex? I'm a married man.

Tom Clancy

Adam and Eve had an ideal marriage. He didn't have to hear about all the men she could have married and she didn't have to hear about the way his mother cooked.

Kimberley Broyles

I don't want to say my girlfriend was loose. I think the term now is 'user-friendly'.

Emo Philips

The only thing that men really do better than women is peeing out a campfire.

Roseanne Barr

Dates used to be made days or even weeks in advance. Now dates tend to be made the day after. You get a phone call from someone who says, 'If anyone asks, I was out to dinner with you last night, okay?'

P.J. O'Rourke

Never assume that a guy understands that you and he have a relationship.

Dave Barry

I broke up with my girlfriend. She moved in with another guy and I draw the line at that.

Gary Shandling

Males cannot look at breasts and think at the same time.

Dave Barry

I think if people marry it ought to be for life; the laws are altogether too lenient with them.

Finley Peter Dunne

I've got to stop taking Viagra because I can't zip up my trousers.

Richard Harris

I practise safe sex. I use an airbag. It's a little startling at first when it flies out. Then the woman realises it's safer than being thrown clear.

Gary Shandling

I love men, even though they're lying, cheating scumbags.

Gwyneth Paltrow

A woman driver is one who drives like a man but gets blamed for it.

Patricia Ledger

Young man, if she asks you if you like her hair that way, beware; the woman has already committed matrimony with you in her heart.

Don Marquis

Not all men fancy eighteen-year-olds; no, many of them fancy sixteen-year-olds.

Kathy Lette

'Personhole' for 'manhole' is not an acceptable de-sexed word.

Shirley Dean

Contrary to what many women believe, it's easy to develop a long-term, intimate and mutually fulfilling relationship with a male. Of course, the male has to be a Labrador retriever.

Dave Barry

The essential difference between men and women is that men think the Three Stooges are funny, and women don't.

Jay Leno

There is some cooperation between wild creatures. The wolf and the stork work the same neighbourhood.

Alexander Woollcott

As soon as I get home, I'm going to rip my wife's bra off – the elastic is killing me.

Roy Brown

A long-forgotten loved one will appear soon. Buy the negatives at any price.

Emo Philips

The weather forecast reminded me of a typical married day of yesteryear. After a bright start it was

going to be cold and dry. The evening would be chilly.

Jeffrey Bernard

Never despise a bow-legged girl. She may be on pleasure bent.

Billy Bennett

I proposed to Neil. It wasn't a question; it was an order.

Christine Hamilton

At least I can wear high heels now.

Nicole Kidman

No bird has a bill as big as the stork's.

Herbert Prochnow

The only real argument for marriage is that it's still the best method of getting acquainted.

Heywood Broun

My best chat-up line was: 'Shall I show you a few of my judo holds?'.

Honor Blackman

Time and tide wait for no man, but time always stands still for the woman of thirty.

Robert Frost

There are perks to being flat chested. I can pass for fourteen in a blackout.

Jenny Eclair

At what age are men most attractive to women? Four years old.

Bill Vaughan

My divorce came as a complete surprise to me. That will happen when you haven't been home in eighteen years.

Lee Trevis

The only man who thinks Phyllis Diller is a ten is a shoe salesman.

Bob Hope

In lovemaking, what Tom Arnold lacked in size, he made up for in speed.

Roseanne Barr

Even a 747 looks small when it lands in the Grand Canyon.

Tom Arnold

Give me a sixteen-year-old and I'll return him when he's twenty-one.

Mae West

There are two theories about how to argue with a woman. Neither one works.

Walter Matthau

Poor Elizabeth Taylor – always the bride, never the bridesmaid.

Richard Curtis

If you could see my legs when I take my boots off, you'd form some idea of what unrequited affection is.

Charles Dickens

I still miss my ex-wife, but my aim is improving.

Henny Youngman

I genuinely do not believe in divorce.

Elizabeth Taylor

During lovemaking last night, Natasha called my name. I immediately ran into the bedroom to see what she wanted.

Karl McDermott

An engagement in war is a battle. In love it is the salubrious calm that precedes the real hostilities.

Gideon Wurdz

He kissed her hand with a sound like a mackerel being replaced clumsily on a fishmonger's slab, and withdrew.

J.B. Morton

I nearly had a psychic girlfriend once, but she left me before we met.

Steven Wright

Life with Zsa Zsa Gabor was like living on the slopes of a volcano. Very pleasant between eruptions.

George Sanders

I married Frank Sinatra because what would it have looked like if I didn't?

Ava Gardner

She said she would marry me over her dead body and I held her to that promise.

Emo Philips

The most important thing a woman can have –
next to talent of course – is her hairdresser.

Joan Crawford

I once heard an alpha male say that sex with an
older woman was like throwing a banana down
Oxford Street.

Vanessa Wilde

If Mr Laughton is not a lady, why does he have breasts?

Igor Ustinov

In California, handicapped parking is for women
who are frigid.

Joan Rivers

I am a drag queen trapped in a woman's body.

Kylie Minogue

Normally I have to keep the eager totty back with a
shitty stick.

A.A. Gill

My marriage lasted just ten months. We still had
wedding cake left.

Frank Skinner

My wife had half-a-dozen sex change operations, but couldn't find anything she liked.

Woody Allen

If Jeremy Clarkson came across a homosexual in his bath he would jump on the loo seat holding his nightshirt tightly at the knees and call in desperate falsetto for his wife to come and deal with the huge hairy thing.

A.A. Gill

I asked a beautiful girl if I could see her home. She showed me a photo of it.

Tony Blackburn

Oh, I'm so clever! I wish I could sleep with myself.

Philip O'Connor

Marriage is like having to stand on one leg for the rest of your life.

Philip Larkin

I picked a pansy in the garden of love.

Sophie Tucker

There are some sure-fire ways to tell if your date is too young for you. Can he fly for half-fare? Are his love letters to you written in crayon? Do his pyjamas have feet? When you ask him a question does he raise his hand before answering?

Phyllis Diller

It is okay to laugh in the bedroom so long as you don't point.

Will Durst

A wife is someone who gladly shares half your bed, but claims her half in the middle.

William Tallon

A real woman has a special attitude to money. If she earns money, it is hers; if her husband earns it, it is theirs.

Joyce Jillsons

Some of the best homosexuals are my friends.

Alan Brien

♥

I don't know anything about Jayne Mansfield except the common gossip I heard. When it comes to men, I hear she never turns anything down except the bedcovers.

Mae West

Index

Other titles by Des MacHale:

Wit
Wit Hits the Spot
Wit on Target
Wit: The Last Laugh
Wit Rides Again
Ultimate Wit
Ready Wit
Irish Wit
Wisdom

Other humorous compilations published by Prion:

Chick Wit
Cynic's Dictionary
Fathers' Wit
Funny Money
High Society
Hollywood Wit
Jewish Humour
The Ruling Asses
Wisecracks
Women's Wicked Wit
More Women's Wicked Wit
Wrinklies' Wit & Wisdom